CONNOISSEUR KIDS

For our Connoisseur Kids:
Arabella, Georgina, William, and Thomas

Library of Congress Cataloging-in-Publication Data:

Names: Scott, Jennifer L. (Jennifer Lynn), author. | Owen, Clare,
  illustrator.

Title: Connoisseur kids / by Jennifer L. Scott ; illustrations by Clare Owen.

Other titles: Corrected title: Connoisseur kids : etiquette, manners, and
  living well for little ones

Description: San Francisco : Chronicle Books, [2019]

Identifiers: LCCN 2018034515 | ISBN 9781452173474 (hc : alk. paper)

Subjects: LCSH: Etiquette for children and teenagers--Handbooks, manuals,
  etc. | Child rearing--Handbooks, manuals, etc. | LCGFT: Handbooks and
  manuals.

Classification: LCC BJ1857.C5 S347 2019 | DDC 395.1/22--dc23 LC record available at
  https://lccn.loc.gov/2018034515

Manufactured in China.

Design by Anne Kenady.
Typeset by Frank Brayton.

10 9 8 7 6 5 4 3 2 1

Chronicle books and gifts are available at special quantity
discounts to corporations, professional associations, literacy
programs, and other organizations. For details and discount
information, please contact our premiums department at
corporatesales@chroniclebooks.com or at 1-800-759-0190.

Chronicle Books LLC
680 Second Street
San Francisco, California 94107
www.chroniclebooks.com

CONNOISSEUR KIDS

Etiquette,
Manners, and
Living Well
for Parents
and Their
Little Ones

JENNIFER L. SCOTT
bestselling author of the Madame Chic series

ILLUSTRATIONS BY CLARE OWEN

CHRONICLE BOOKS
SAN FRANCISCO

Contents

INTRODUCTION

Life as a kid is so exciting. Kids are constantly learning new things and experiencing fresh adventures. Life can be daunting, too, as we are expected to fit into a world that has a lot of rules.

Kids will learn to answer the following questions, and more! What do you do when you meet someone for the first time? How do you act at the dinner table? What sorts of things do you need to do to stay clean and take care of your body? Is it even possible to keep your room tidy for more than one day? How do you express yourself when you are feeling angry? There are so many pressing questions, and when kids get these answers, they can put them into action and start to enjoy everyday adventures with confidence and joy.

This book is about becoming a Connoisseur Kid. What is a Connoisseur Kid? To answer that, let's first look at what a connoisseur is. A *connoisseur* is defined as an expert judge in matters of taste. It means that there is a certain field that you know so well that you are an expert in it! If you love art and have studied it well, you could be a connoisseur of fine art, for example. If you love to ride horses, have spent a lot of time around them, know how to care for them, and know what makes them unique, you could be a connoisseur of horses.

Connoisseur Kids become experts in the art of living. Being a kid is one of the most wonderful phases of life. Adults always look back at their childhood to reminisce about, or think back to, their fondest memories. Connoisseur Kids enjoy everything that goes along with being young and gain many new skills that will carry them into adulthood with ease.

The skills kids will learn regarding etiquette, manners, tidiness, hygiene (keeping your body clean), health, and thinking of others will fit beautifully into everyday life, helping to guide each day. Have fun jumping right in to explore these topics. This book is also full of unique crafts, recipes, games, and challenges that will keep you and yours busy and inspire you to share with others.

How to Use This Book

This book is meant to be read with both child and parent, together, or to be used as a script for parents to share this information with their kids. Spend quality time with family as you delve into each chapter and challenge. If your kids are old enough to read this book by themselves, allow them to do so, or have them read out loud to the family. If not, enjoy reading together. The activities in this book will challenge kids, hopefully make them laugh, and activate their enthusiasm for living well.

Embark on an exciting journey of newness and discovery as you uncover what it truly means to be a Connoisseur Kid... starting now.

Etiquette: What Is It?

Etiquette is polite behavior. It's how we act in front of people and also by ourselves. Etiquette is very important. Can you imagine a world without etiquette? Having no rules might sound fun at first, kind of like one big party! But think about it: a world with no rules and no manners would be a very unpleasant place to live. No one would say "please" or "thank you." People would just grab something if they wanted it. Cutting in line would be totally normal. A world without etiquette would leave everyone very frustrated, indeed!

The word *etiquette* comes from France way back in the 1600s. *Etiquette* meant to keep off the grass at the royal court. It was a code of conduct that everyone was expected to follow. Well, just like they followed etiquette in the royal French courts hundreds of years ago, we will strive to follow it today. Etiquette doesn't have to be stuffy or intimidating; it can actually be fun to practice! And, don't worry, you won't be learning it alone: your entire family is going to practice with you! So, let's get started with the area where your manners will shine the most: when you communicate.

1

COMMUNICATION

Parents, the goals in this chapter are to: 1. Learn how to best communi-cate; 2. Practice good communication skills on a daily basis; and 3. Enjoy communicating with others.

Communication is the exchange of information with other people. It is also a means of connection with others. We are going to start with communication because our days are framed by communicating with other people. As Connoisseur Kids, we want to live harmoniously with others and be effective communicators. This chapter will give you tips and techniques on how to make your communication skills shine!

EYE CONTACT

When learning about proper communication, there's a major skill we need to master first: eye contact! Do you know what eye contact is? It's when you look someone in the eyes when you're talking to them. It's important to make eye contact not only when you're talking but also when you're listening.

When you make eye contact with the person you're talking to, you make that person feel really special. You each know that you're being heard because you are giving that person your full attention by looking at them.

Using eye contact might feel awkward at first. That means you might feel funny looking into the eyes of the person to whom you're talking. But if you practice enough, it will come naturally to you. Practice with your family. When your mom is talking to you, for example, look her in the eyes. When you're asking her a question, look her in the eyes. Do the same with your dad. Even your brothers, sisters, and cousins! You might not be used to it, but it can be fun to look at people in the eyes.

Whenever someone talks to you,
Look them in the eyes.
It lets them know you're listening.
You will feel very wise!
When you're the one who's talking
And relaying a little fact,
Nothing feels more special
Than when they give you eye contact!

THE EYE CONTACT GAME

ITEMS NEEDED:
Sticky notes
Pencils

How to play: You will need a partner to play this game. Each person takes several sticky notes and writes the name of a thing on each note. Examples could be a lamp, bed, stove, chair, doll, fork, computer, cat, etc. If you're playing with younger players who can't read yet, you can always draw a picture of the thing rather than writing the word.

Now trade sticky notes, but don't look at what is written on yours! Stick the note on your forehead. Go to your partner and take turns. You are going to ask them questions to figure out what you are. For example, let's say your sticky note says "lamp." Your conversation with the other person as you try to guess what you are might go like this:

Player 1: "Am I in the kitchen?"
Player 2: "No."
Player 1: "Am I in the living room?"
Player 2: "Yes."
Player 1: "Do you sit on me?"
Player 2: "No."
Player 1: "Do I light up?"
Player 2: "Yes!"
Player 1: "Am I a lamp?"
Player 2: "Yes!"

It's fun to try to guess what you are, but there is a twist to this game! The entire time you are asking or answering questions, you must maintain eye contact with your partner. It's OK to blink, but if you look down, or away, your turn is over and your partner gets to start guessing. Play the game until you have used all of the sticky notes. You will quickly become accustomed to maintaining eye contact in a conversation with this fun game.

- CONNOISSEUR KIDS ASSIGNMENT -

PRACTICE EYE CONTACT

Work on maintaining good eye contact today with everyone you come across. Practice on your family first. Notice how you are able to listen better when you practice good eye contact. Also notice how it feels nice when people look you in the eyes when you're talking to them.

POSTURE

P osture is how we sit, stand, and carry ourselves. You might wonder what posture has to do with communication and manners, but it plays a very important role. This is because we not only communicate with our words and our eyes, but with our bodies, too.

Try this activity to see what I mean. Stand in front of a mirror and slouch. Make your slouch exaggerated: hunch your shoulders, stick out your neck, let your head drop, and jut out your stomach. How do you look? Do you look happy or sad? Lazy or energetic? Do you look like you're having a good day or a bad day?

Now try standing with good posture. Straighten up your back, let your shoulders drop, put your chin up, and tuck your stomach in. Pretend you're being held up by a string like you're a marionette puppet. Now how do you look? Do you look happy or sad? Lazy or energetic? Like you're having a good day or a bad day?

Do you see how your posture can communicate things to other people? If you're slouching throughout your day, you might appear sluggish, lazy, and unhappy. But if you're standing straight, you appear ready for anything, upbeat and energetic!

Throughout the day,
Stand straight and tall.
This posture says,
You're giving it your all!
Don't hunch over
In your chair.
Instead sit straight
To show you care!

- CONNOISSEUR KIDS ASSIGNMENT -

MAINTAIN GOOD POSTURE

Your assignment today is to use your best posture. Whether you're standing up or sitting in a chair, make yourself straight and tall. You'll notice you have more energy. It's a great feeling! Practice good posture today and every day.

TISSUE DANCE GAME
(FOR GREAT POSTURE)

This game can be played with only one or two people, but the more the merrier, so gather your siblings, parents, and friends together.

ITEMS NEEDED:
1 tissue or lightweight, silky scarf per person
A wide-open space
Music

How to play: Have everyone place one tissue on top of their head. Start the music. Players can dance to the music in whatever way they like. The goal is to keep the tissue on your head. If the tissue starts to drop, you can pick it up, but if it falls on the floor, you are out and must watch the rest of the game. The last person standing wins! This game teaches you to hold your head high and have good posture, even when you're doing something active and being silly!

SPEAKING CLEARLY

D o you know what *communication* is? The dictionary says it's "the exchange of information or news." That's a fancy way to say it's how people talk to each other.

There are many more ways to communicate than talking to each other. In addition to words, you can communicate through writing, actions, and facial expressions. Good communication is an important skill to have! In this section, we are going to learn how to communicate well. You will be amazed at how smoothly your day will go when you learn to communicate well.

The first step to communicating well is speaking clearly. Have you ever heard someone mumble? Their head is usually down, they aren't looking at you, and they say something so quietly that you can't understand. It's frustrating to talk to someone who is mumbling!

MUMBLE EXERCISE

Try this exercise: Mumble something to your parent and see if they can guess what you are saying. Now have them mumble something to you. This game will probably make you laugh, but think about how hard it would be if every time you talked to someone you couldn't understand what that person was saying! As good communicators, we should aim to speak clearly and let our voice ring out like a bell. Now try saying what you were trying to say in your clearest voice. Sit up straight, look the other person in the eyes, and say your sentence. There, that's better! Here is another exercise you can do to help you speak clearly.

TONGUE TWISTERS

It's fun to say tongue twisters. Practice saying them with a clear voice. Face a partner as you each say the tongue twisters to each other. Or try looking in the mirror as you say them so you can see how you're communicating.

Do drop in at the Dewdrop Inn.
A proper copper coffee pot.
Six slippery snails slid slowly seaward.
Fred fed Ted bread and Ted fed Fred bread.
Crisp crusts crackle and crunch.
Which wristwatches are Swiss wristwatches?
A box of mixed biscuits, a mixed biscuit box.

PRACTICE SPEAKING CLEARLY

Today, your assignment is to speak clearly every time you talk. Try not to mumble. *Enunciate*, or clearly say, each word just as you did during the tongue twister exercise. Let your voice ring out like a bell. With daily practice, you will be speaking clearly as a regular habit.

- SPOTLIGHT ON -

ALEXANDER GRAHAM BELL

Alexander Graham Bell (1847–1922) was a Scottish-born scientist who is famous for inventing the telephone in 1876 and organizing the Bell Telephone Company in 1877. Mr. Bell also devoted his life to helping the deaf, establishing the American Association to Promote the Teaching of Speech to the Deaf in 1890. Mr. Bell died peacefully on August 2, 1922, at his home in Nova Scotia, Canada. Upon his death, the whole telephone system shut down for one minute as a tribute to his life and work. Alexander Graham Bell was a major innovator in the world of communication.

Saying "Please"

Now that we are speaking clearly, using good eye contact, and having great posture, we feel ready for anything! Let's get into details and talk about the actual words we say. Everyone knows that saying "please" and "thank you" is important. You say "please" when you would like something and "thank you" when you receive it. "Please" is often referred to as the "magic" word because, without it, you might have a hard time getting what you want.

Just imagine a world where no one says "please." You would hear people saying "Give me that!" and "I want it now!" Neither of these phrases is pleasing to the ears. They are pretty harsh. It shouldn't come as a surprise to know that saying "please" is also pleasing to the ears. That's part of its magic. Saying "please" can change a yucky phrase like "Give me the scissors!" to a pleasant one: "May I please have the scissors?"

When you take the time to say please,
It puts people at ease.

Remember to say "please" any time you ask for something, no matter how big or how small it is. Saying "please" adds sweetness to your request. You can see that by studying the good vs. bad manners chart below.

GOOD MANNERS	BAD MANNERS
"May I please have some ice cream?"	"I want some ice cream!"
"Can you please pass the broccoli?"	"Give me the broccoli!"
"Could you please open this for me?"	"Open this for me!"
"Will you please help me with my math homework?"	"Help me with this math homework."

When you say "please," be sure to use your new skills by saying it clearly and using eye contact.

Saying "Thank You"

Saying "thank you" is one of the most important things you can say because it expresses your gratitude. A heartfelt "thank you" goes a long way and reminds you of what you are grateful for. You will say "thank you" to everyone: your parents, your teacher, a waiter at a restaurant, a nice lady who holds a door open for you. There are many ways to say "thank you." You can say "thank you" by speaking it, you can show thanks by a warm smile, and you can give thanks by writing a thank-you card. Let's look at the three different ways here.

Speaking a "Thank You"

Let's practice speaking clearly with eye contact when we say our thank you. Try this activity with your parent or sibling: Have them give you a pretend gift. It can be anything from a stuffed animal in the room to a pencil from your desk. Take the "gift" and, with your head hanging low, mumble "thank you" without looking at them. How did that make you feel? Ask your parent how it made them feel. Did they feel their gift was appreciated?

Now try it again, this time letting your "thank you" ring loud as a bell. Look them in the eyes and smile as you say it. How did you feel after that? I bet your parent felt very special! Remember to always speak your "thank you" loud and clear, and with eye contact for the best delivery.

GRATITUDE LIST

Write down 10 things you're grateful for. Share this list with your family by gathering everyone together. You can read it in front of them like a performance. Make sure you have good posture when you're speaking; it will make the delivery of your words even more special! And, of course, make sure you read your list in a clear voice. When you are finished, why not ask your family members what they are grateful for, too?

1

2

3

4

5

6

7

8

9

10

The Ultimate Holiday of Thanks, Thanksgiving

On the fourth Thursday of November, Americans celebrate Thanksgiving, the ultimate holiday of thanks. We gather with family and friends around a special feast and give thanks for the blessings we have in our lives. Gratitude for family, friends, and food is so important. What is your favorite part about Thanksgiving? What's your favorite thing to eat at the Thanksgiving table?

Thank You with a Smile

Sometimes you aren't able to voice your "thank you," so you will express your gratitude by acknowledging the other person with a smile and perhaps a nod. You might have seen your parents do this in the car. If another driver lets your car go first, your mom or dad might wave and smile to the other person. They're saying "thank you" with their wave.

When you're not able to say "thank you" out loud, you can always say "thank you" with your actions. A smile, a nod, and a wave will go far to communicate your gratitude. Can you think of a time when you thanked someone with your smile?

Thank-You Notes

Another way to express thanks is through written words. When you receive a gift from someone, always remember to send a thank-you note. You can craft the card yourself, which makes it even more special. If you don't like to draw, a letter of thanks is just fine. The recipient of the card will be thrilled with your thoughtfulness and feel very appreciated indeed.

There are many different ways you can do this. Normally, when you write a thank-you note, you address the person who has given you the gift. You say "thank you for the gift" and one or two things about why you like the gift. Then you can close the letter by signing your name. Here's an example:

Dear Aunt Emmy,
   Thank you for the snow globe you sent me for my birthday. I love to shake it and watch the snow fall on the house. It reminds me of my favorite season, winter!
   With love,
   Olivia

Now it's your turn. Practice writing a thank-you note on the lines of the next page. Thank a family member who has done something nice for you recently.

Always start off your thank-you note addressing the person you're writing to. You do this by writing "Dear" and then their name, followed by a comma. Then write "thank you" and why you love their gift and are grateful for it. You can sign your name any number of ways. Here are some examples:

With love,
Sincerely,
Yours truly,
Love,
Best regards,
Best wishes,
Warm regards,
With appreciation,

When writing to a close family member, like your grandmother, for example, the best closer to use is "with love" or "love." When writing to a non-family member, use "sincerely" or "yours truly," or any of the others on the list.

_____ ,

_____ ,

3 THANK-YOU CARD CRAFTS

WATERCOLOR CARD

Prepare a few thank-you cards in advance and give them a personal touch by painting them with watercolors. Gather some white cardstock or heavy watercolor paper. Cut out at least five cards. On the front of the card, let your artistry flow with watercolors. Paint anything you like! Leave the inside blank for writing. On the back, paint another small picture or create your own "bar code" with a pen to mimic a card you'd buy in a shop. Let them dry, and you have instant personalized cards to send off the next time you receive a gift.

WRAPPING PAPER CARD

There are always scraps of wrapping paper left over at the end of the holiday season. Recycle these pieces by turning them into nice thank-you cards! Cut cardstock out of heavy paper, and glue the scraps artistically on the front of your card. Leave a border if you wish, or cut a border out in a complementary color from colored paper. Keep your festive cards handy. You know you'll need them after the holiday season is over to thank people for the presents you've received.

DRIED FLOWER CARD

Go in the garden and pick some flowers. Lavender and roses work best. Hang your flowers upside down to dry them for one week. When they are dry, you can take the petals from the flowers and glue them to cardstock. Allow this to dry fully. These make beautiful cards and will be such a delight to whoever opens them.

Thank-you note tip: Write a thank-you note right after you've opened a gift. That way, you won't forget or put it off too long.

> Write a note of thanks,
> After you receive a gift.
> Right away, don't delay!
> Act now, be swift!
> Tomorrow you might forget,
> The next day will fly by.
> Write your note of thanks.
> Go on, don't be shy!

When You're Mad, Give Thanks!

Have you ever had one of those downright horrible days? It might feel like everything is going wrong. You stepped in a puddle and your socks are wet the whole day, someone said something mean to you at school, your sister made you angry by pushing you aside to get into the car, you ran out of ice pops at home . . . as you can see, this is a very bad day! Well, when you're having one of these days, the best way to combat it is by focusing on what you are thankful for. There's always something. You can be thankful for having food to eat and a bed to sleep in. You could be thankful for your dog that comforts you when you are sad or your favorite book series. You could be thankful for your mom's warm hug. You could be thankful for just being alive!

It's not the first place your thoughts will go when you're mad, but you can train them to go there. If it helps, keep a little gratitude journal by your bed where you can jot down everything you are grateful for. If you're having one of those days where you can't even remember what you're grateful for, you can pull out your journal and read the list. You'll feel better when you finish. Sometimes we can get into a funk when everything seems to be going wrong and focus on all the bad things happening to us. When you shift your focus to what you are happy and grateful for, you flip your bad day on its head!

Saying "You're Welcome"

We know how to say "please" when we would like something, and "thank you" when we get it, but what about when you're the one who does something nice for someone else? When someone says "thank you" to you, you can say "you're welcome" back.

Another way to say "you're welcome" is "my pleasure!" This means that you have enjoyed helping the other person. You could also say "no problem!" Saying "you're welcome" means you have received their thanks and the deal is done. "You're welcome" is the pretty bow on the package.

DIFFERENT WAYS TO SAY "PLEASE," "THANK YOU," AND "YOU'RE WELCOME" AROUND THE WORLD

ENGLISH	FRENCH	SPANISH	JAPANESE	CHINESE	ITALIAN
Please	s'il vous plaît	por favor	onegaishimasu	qǐng	per favore
Thank you	merci	gracias	arigatō	xièxiè	grazie
You're welcome	de rien	de nada	dōitashimashite	bù kèqì	prego

When you do something nice for someone
And they thank you for good measure,
Always say "you're welcome" back,
"no problem," or "my pleasure!"

Greetings

You will greet people all throughout your day. "Hello" is the most common greeting, but it's nice to use others, too. "Good morning," "good afternoon," and "good evening" are fun to use. The key with greetings is to say them clearly and use that eye contact you have been practicing.

It's very polite to ask someone how he or she is doing. You can often add this to your greeting: "Good morning, Mr. Williams. How are you?" If you want to get really fancy, you can say, "How do you do?" Casual ways to ask others how they are doing are "How's it going?" and "What's up?" You can use these greetings with your peers, but try the more formal ones when addressing adults and new acquaintances. The more formal greetings convey respect, and we should always show respect to our elders.

GREETINGS AROUND THE WORLD

ENGLISH	FRENCH	SPANISH	JAPANESE	CHINESE	ITALIAN
hello	bonjour	hola	kon'nichiwa	nìn hǎo	ciao
good morning	bonjour	buenos días	ohayōgozaimasu	zǎo'ān	buon giorno
good afternoon	bonne après-midi	buenas tardes	kon'nichiwa	wǔ'ān	buon pomeriggio
good evening	bonsoir	buena noches	konbanwa	wǎnshàng hǎo	buona sera
goodbye	au revoir	adiós	sayōnara	zàijiàn	arrivederci

How to Interrupt Someone Politely

Thinking of others doesn't always mean helping them or doing something nice for them. It's about showing them respect, too. When we put others before ourselves, sometimes we have to put what we want on hold. What about when you have something you really want to ask your parents, but they are in a conversation with each other? In other words, what's the best way to interrupt their conversation with each other? If it's an emergency, you can interrupt the conversation right away. For example, your dog just escaped and ran down the street. You can interrupt their conversation to tell them that. If your request is not an emergency, let's say you'd like some ice cream or you'd like to see if you can play with the neighbors, you should wait patiently until there is a pause in their conversation. Then you say, "Excuse me, may I have some ice cream?" or "Excuse me, may I please play with the neighbors?" Waiting for a pause in the conversation, then saying "excuse me" is a polite way to interrupt.

A GOOD HANDSHAKE

When you meet someone for the first time, your new acquaintance might shake your hand. Practice having a good handshake and you will feel confident when meeting new people. The key to a good handshake is one of the skills you've already acquired: eye contact! When you're shaking someone's hand, look them in the eyes at the same time with a warm smile. Typically, everyone shakes with their right hand. Even if you are left-handed, you will probably shake with your right hand. Hold out your hand and lock hands with the other person; your thumbs will be on top and your other fingers beneath. Your grip should be firm but not too strong. Pump your handshake three times while maintaining eye contact with the other person. After three shakes, you can let go. Practice your firm handshake now with your mom or dad.

COMMUNICATING YOUR FEELINGS

Our new communication skills will help us with everyday challenges and interactions, such as meeting new people and communicating with friends, teachers, and family members. What do we do when we need to communicate more difficult things, such as our feelings?

It's pretty easy to communicate when you're feeling happy. You laugh, you dance, you jump, you sing, you tell people why you're on top of the world. When our emotions take a turn, however, it's more difficult to communicate what we are feeling. You might feel sad and upset, and want to express that, but just end up crying and not being able to get your words out. If that happens to you, that's OK! It's good to cry when you're upset; don't hold it in. But when you're through crying, how can you convey your emotions to people? When you feel sad, don't bottle it up and keep it to yourself. Share it with someone. Tell your mom or dad or siblings how you're feeling. Communicating your feelings is a healthy thing to do.

What about when you're just plain mad? This could be the hardest time to communicate. When you were a little kid, you probably communicated your anger through tantrums. Have you ever seen toddlers throw a tantrum when they don't get their way? They scream and kick and flail their arms. Sometimes they throw themselves on the floor and roll around dramatically. Maybe you have a little brother or sister who does this. Sometimes when you're watching one of these tantrums, all you want to do is laugh. Why? Because their reaction is so silly and dramatic! But before we laugh at their tantrums, we should look at our own ways of communicating when we get mad. We may not throw ourselves on the floor in fits of screams anymore, but when we're angry, we probably don't communicate our anger in the best way.

If you brother angers you, for example, you might kick or push him or snatch something from his hands to anger him back. None of these are healthy ways of communicating anger. When you feel angry, like steam is going to come out of your ears, the best thing to do is pause. Why pause? When you get angry, you might have what's called a knee-jerk reaction.

What is a knee-jerk reaction? Have you ever been to the doctor where they tap your knee gently with a rubber mallet? If your knee was tapped in the proper place, your leg probably shot out without you even knowing it. You experienced a knee jerk.

In the same way, our angry reaction can happen quickly and, before you know it, you've done something you regret. You might hit someone or scream or throw something. If you were in your normal state of being, you wouldn't do that. So pause when you are mad. Take several deep breaths. Go drink a glass of water.

You can even cry. It's better to pause than to express anger in a way that you will regret.

After you've calmed down, you can go deal with the other person. You can calmly explain to them why you are upset. Your brother will be more likely to listen to you if you are calm and not angry. It's normal to feel angry, but the trick is how you process it. Pause. Take a break. Blow off steam. Then go back to the situation to resolve it in a calm way.

- CONNOISSEUR KIDS ASSIGNMENT -

USE ALL YOUR COMMUNICATION SKILLS

Become a connoisseur of communication. You have learned so many skills in this chapter, everything from speaking clearly with eye contact to expressing gratitude and feelings. Let every situation that comes to you be met with clear communication. Once you learn to communicate, so many doors will open for you in life. You will do better in school, you will have less conflict, and you will appear confident and trustworthy. Have fun combining all of the elements of these lessons and applying them to your everyday life. Older people will marvel at how well spoken you are for a young person. Your actions will assure them you are a Connoisseur Kid!

2

TABLE MANNERS

Parents, the goals in this chapter are to: 1. Learn about table manners;
2. Practice them at every meal; and 3. Enjoy every meal with others.

Knowing how to have good manners, and putting those manners into action, will put you at ease in many situations. We are used to eating meals at home: breakfast, lunch, snacks, and dinner. But there are times when we eat meals outside of the home: at school, when we go to restaurants, and when we are invited to eat at a friend or family member's house. When we practice good table manners at home, we are able to bring them "on the road" with us, as well, and be comfortable in any dining situation.

You might wonder why you need table manners . . . when it seems like no one else has them. If you are at a table with a lot of other kids and they are breaking all the rules, you might just want to join in so you can fit in. Be a good example here. Be known for your impeccable table manners no matter what the other people around you are doing. They may just wonder what is so special about you.

- CONNOISSEUR KIDS TIP -

ALWAYS ASK TO HELP

Before any meal, always ask how you can help. There are so many ways that you can be useful. You might need to round up the rest of your family to let them know it's time to eat. You might grate some cheese or stir a sauce to help prepare the meal. You might need to wipe the table before everyone sits down. It might be your job to turn off the TV and put on some music. You could also pour the water. You could even be asked to set the table! Before each meal, always ask how you can help, and you will be given an important job every time.

SETTING THE TABLE

Setting the table is a great way to help your parents get ready for dinner. It can be quite fun, too, because you get to be creative. There are so many ways to set a table! You could use place mats, a tablecloth, or both together. You could use cloth napkins or paper napkins, and choosing which plates to use is always fun, too.

Everything depends on what you're having for dinner. If you're having chili, for example, you'll need bowls for the chili and a side plate for the salad and cornbread. If you're having a more casual dinner, such as pizza, you'll need a plate and a napkin. View table settings as a fun challenge. Aim to make the table look as nice as possible. A beautifully set table will make the dinner experience special. It doesn't have to be fancy or complicated. An easy rule to remember is that forks always go to the left of the plate and knives and spoons go on the right of the plate. Place the silverware in order of use, with the first items you'll be

using on the outside. That way, you can work your way in as you dine. Follow this guide below and you will have many ideas for setting the table.

Standard table setting:

Set a place mat on the table in front of each seat. Put the dinner plate on top of the place mat and a salad plate on top of the dinner plate. Place the napkin to the left of the plate. (The napkin may also be placed on top of the plates, if using a special napkin fold or ring.) Place the fork on the left of the plate, and a knife on the right of the plate. Place the drink cup at the top right of the place setting.

Setting the table for a soup or chili dinner:

Set a place mat or tablecloth on the table. Set a large bowl for soup or chili at each place setting. Place a side dish (for cornbread or salad) off the side to the left. Place the drink cup at the top right. Place the napkin to the left of the bowl. Place a fork on the left (for salad or a side dish) and your spoon on the right.

Arranging Flowers for the Dinner Table

If Mom and Dad need help styling the dinner table, you can offer to arrange the flowers. The secret to a great table arrangement is to make it low. If you're having a conversation with someone across the table from you, you want to be able to see their face, not a giant display of flowers.

The key to keeping it low is to use a short vase, not a tall one. Find a short vase and fill it with water. Then go into the yard and cut flowers and foliage that fit into the vase (ask Mom or Dad first, of course!). You might have to trim the stem a few times to get it right. Wear garden gloves when you are cutting roses so you don't get pricked by thorns.

If your garden does not have any flowers because of the season, you can always get creative and pick pretty greenery. Evergreen branches and red berries make for a pretty arrangement in the winter. Get creative with your low flower arrangement. The whole family will appreciate your beautiful contribution to the dinner table.

NAPKIN RING

Using napkin rings is a great way to style your table. You don't need to go buy napkin rings in the store—you can make them yourself! Here are three ideas.

Ribbon napkin ring:
Simply tie a bow around the folded napkin with a piece of ribbon or twine. You have an instant, elegant napkin ring.

Treasure napkin ring:
When you finish with a roll of paper towels, save the inside tube. Cut the tube into six to eight smaller rings that are even in size. You can now use these as the base for your napkin ring. Paint these cardboard rings and then glue a "treasure" onto it such as a small seashell or dried flower.

Beaded napkin ring:
You will need beads, a thin wire, and scissors. Cut a piece of wire about 6 inches [15 cm] long. Create a small loop at the end of your wire and secure it by wrapping the wire around itself a few times. Now string the beads in a nice pattern down the wire. They should stop at the loop. Leave 1 inch [2.5 cm] at the other end of the wire. Circle it around and twist the end of the wire around the loop until the beads are secure in a napkin ring shape.

Folding Napkins

Have you ever visited a fancy restaurant and noticed how they fold the napkins? Sometimes napkins are folded like roses, sometimes like swans. Sometimes they are even folded to look like the Sydney Opera House in Australia! Napkin folding is fun to do, and when you learn a few different easy ways to do it, you can make your table look special. Here are three easy napkin-folding techniques.

The pocket fold:
Lay your napkin out flat on a table. Fold it in half and then in half again. It should now look like a square. Take the top layer of the open end and fold it down so that its tip is now on top of the folded corner of the napkin. Now fold the napkin into thirds lengthwise. Turn the napkin around and you have a pocket to place a knife and fork in.

The fan fold:
Lay your napkin flat on a table. Now fold it like an accordion. Secure the bottom third with a ribbon or one of the napkin rings you made. Fan out the accordion fold as you lay the napkin down on the plate.

The bow fold:
Fold your napkin into a rectangular shape and secure the center with a ribbon, or one of the napkin rings you made. Now fan out either side and lay it horizontally on your plate. This looks like a large bow.

SITTING AT
THE TABLE

Now that you're sitting at your nicely set table, there are a few etiquette tips to keep in mind.

Tip number one is to wait until everyone is seated and served before you start eating. You might be the first one at the table. Your enthusiasm is great! But to be polite, you want to wait until everyone is seated and has their food before you begin eating yours. Wait patiently until everyone is served and then you can all begin at the same time. Otherwise, you might finish your meal long before someone else.

Tip number two is to never chew with your mouth open or talk with your mouth full. When you chew your food, chew slowly. If you need to talk, wait until you've swallowed before speaking. If you've ever seen anyone chew with their mouth open, you'll know that it's not very pleasant to look at. Never rush yourself. You can always speak after you've swallowed your bite.

Tip number three is to always ask for something to be passed to you. If the salt is out of reach, never lean over the table to grab it; ask the person who is closest to the salt to please pass it to you. The same goes for wanting more food or pouring more water. Any time you need anything that is not easily within your reach, politely ask for the item to be passed to you. For example, you would say, "Dad, can you please pass the salt?" and "Thank you."

Tip number four is to sit still while you're eating. When you wiggle at the dinner table, it's not only distracting for other people but also dangerous! When you're chewing your food, you should be as still as possible; otherwise, your food could go down the wrong way, and that is very unpleasant. Another bad side effect of wiggling is that you could fall out of your chair.

If you get the wiggles at dinner,
Kindly put them away.
You don't want to choke on your food,
And you don't want to topple your tray.
Worse yet, the wiggles could
Make you fly through thin air,
And the whole table will gasp
As you fall out of your chair.
If you get the wiggles at dinner,
Kindly put them away.
Save them for a more suitable time,
Like when you're out to play!

So if we can't wiggle, how should we sit at the table? Here's where **tip number five** comes in: sit with good posture at the table. We are going to sit up as straight as possible. We are not going to hunch over our plate. You've probably heard the famous rule: no elbows on the table. That rule is referring to your posture. When you have your elbows on the table, you are hunched forward and hovering over your food. Sit up as straight as you can.

Now, many people hover over their food so that they don't spill their food in their lap. That makes sense! But if you lean forward slightly so that you're eating over your plate and not directly over your lap, you will successfully eat your food with good posture and keep it where it needs to be.

Tip number six is to always ask to be excused before leaving the table. You don't want to eat your food and then get up as soon as you are finished. Hang around for the conversation and togetherness that comes from mealtime. Enjoy yourself. Don't be in a rush. When it becomes clear that dinner is nearly over, you can ask your parents, "May I be excused?" It's the polite thing to do.

Tip number seven is to thank the cook. Sharing your gratitude with the cook, whether it was your mom, dad, grandma, grandpa, or someone else, will make them feel appreciated. If you are dining in a restaurant, thank the waiter at the end of the meal. If you are dining at a friend's house, always thank their parents. A lot goes into cooking each meal, and it's important to show your gratitude.

Tip number eight is to take your plate to the sink. You might have additional kitchen duty to help with after dinner, but at the very least, help bring your plate to the kitchen sink. Don't forget to push your chair in when you get up. It helps the house look neater when all of the chairs are pushed in.

After practicing these tips regularly, you will become a pro at them. In fact, you will be a connoisseur of good table manners. Remember, it doesn't matter what others are doing around you; maintain your excellent manners at the table, and you could inspire others to follow your lead.

- CONNOISSEUR KIDS TIP -

WASH YOUR HANDS BEFORE EVERY MEAL

Before you sit down to a meal, always make sure you've washed your hands. Your hands acquire many germs—small organisms that cause disease—throughout the day, and you certainly don't want to eat them! Washing your hands before eating ensures your dining experience will be a clean one.

REVIEW THE TIPS

Review the tips for fantastic table manners every night this week before you eat dinner. Read them out loud to your family so they practice them, too. When your meal is over, review the list as a family to see how everyone did. Make a note of areas you need to improve upon and try again tomorrow.

Tip 1: Wait until everyone is served before you start eating.

Tip 2: Never chew with your mouth open or talk with your mouth full.

Tip 3: If you need something on the other side of the table, ask politely for it to be passed to you. Avoid reaching across the table.

Tip 4: Sit still at dinner. No wiggling, or you might fall out of your chair.

Tip 5: Sit with good posture and keep your elbows off the table.

Tip 6: Always ask to be excused before leaving the table.

Tip 7: Before you leave, thank the cook.

Tip 8: Push your chair in and bring your plate to the sink.

Using Your Napkin at the Table

When you sit down to a meal, you will normally see a napkin at the table. (And if you set the table, chances are the napkins are looking fancy!) But what do you do with the napkin once you sit down? Do you keep it by your plate so you can wipe your face as you need to? Actually, the correct answer is to place the napkin in your lap. It's the first thing you should do when you sit down to eat. It might seem weird to do this at first, but when you practice at each meal, it becomes a habit.

Why do we keep our napkin on our lap? Well, even though you are eating over your plate, you still might drop some food in your lap, and the napkin will catch it. When you need to wipe your face, just bring the napkin up and wipe away. Then place it back down in your lap. Never wipe your face with your sleeve. You don't want to stain your clothes. That's what the napkin is there for—to wipe your face and hands, and to catch food that has gone astray. If you have to get up during the meal to go to the bathroom or fetch something for the table, place your napkin on your chair. When you return, put the napkin back in your lap. Think of the napkin as your friend at dinner that is always with you.

Using a Fork, Knife, and Spoon

Did you know that people in different parts of the world use their fork and knife differently? In America, people hold their forks in their right hand while eating. If you are going to cut your food, you move your fork to your left hand, place the tines (the sharp, pointy parts) down, and cut with a knife in your right hand. After cutting your food, you switch the fork to your right hand and resume eating.

In Europe, people always hold their fork, tines down, in their left hand and their knife in their right hand, not letting go of either for the duration of the meal. No matter how you use your knife and fork, there are a few mannerly rules to remember:

- Avoid waving your knife and fork around while you are talking. Keep them low to your plate.

- Always use your fork or spoon unless you are eating finger foods like a cheeseburger and fries. Even though it might be faster to eat mac 'n' cheese with your hands, for example, always use a fork or spoon. Then you won't get sauce all over your fingers.

- When you are finished eating your entire meal, place the knife and fork side by side on your plate in the 11 o'clock position (as if on a clock).

Cheeseburger and fries	BBQ ribs	Chicken nuggets
Pizza	Nachos	Fruit
Tacos	Sandwich and chips	Carrot sticks
Burrito	Corn on the cob	Artichoke

FOODS THAT SHOULD ALWAYS BE EATEN WITH A FORK OR SPOON

Spaghetti (and all other pasta)	Roast dinners	Rice and grains
Stew and soup	Oatmeal	Yogurt
Salad	Cereal	Peas

Do I Have to Eat That? Quiz

Sometimes you are served food you know you don't like. Sometimes you are served food you have never seen before. What do you do in these situations? What about when you want seconds? What about when you want to leave? Take this quiz to test your mannerly knowledge on these tricky occasions.

1. You are served a dish that you know you don't like. The best response is to:

a) Pucker your face and show disgust.

b) Make gagging noises.

c) Avoid eating the food you don't like, but don't make a big deal about it and still be thankful to the cook.

2. You are served something that you have never seen before. You:

a) Exclaim, "Yuck! What is that thing, anyway?"

b) Push your plate away from you dramatically.

c) Try the new food. Who knows, you might like it!

3. Your meal was delicious, and you would like more food. What should you do?

a) Get up and fill your plate again.

b) Shout out, "More please!"

c) Ask, "May I please have more food?"

4. You are finished eating and want to leave the table. What do you do?

a) Get up and leave.

b) Wait until someone else finishes and then leave.

c) Ask, "May I be excused?"

5. You accidentally let out a large burp at the dinner table. You:

a) Giggle uncontrollably.

b) Belt out another burp to see if you can top the last one.

c) Say, "Excuse me."

If you answered c to all of the above questions, you have scored an A+ on your table manners knowledge. The key here is to always think about others as well as yourself. When Mom or Dad takes the time to cook a meal for the family, showing gratitude is always important, even if you don't like the food. When asking for seconds or asking to be excused, we should use our best manners, even if we are just talking to our family. Set a good example at home and when you are out in public eating with others.

Guests

Having guests over for dinner can be very exciting. Whether it's Grandma and Grandpa or family friends, be extra helpful during these times, and Mom and Dad will appreciate you. Now is the moment to let your good manners truly shine!

When you have guests over, you can ask them if they would like anything or if you can get anything for them. Ask them questions about their life and listen to their stories. Enjoy the new guest at the dinner table. Don't ask to be excused early, but rather stay and enjoy the guests' company. Your guests will take note and will always want to come back to visit.

DINNER CONVERSATION

One of the best parts about dinnertime is talking with your family. Mealtimes are not just about eating, but about togetherness, too. Share your stories from the day: the good, the bad, and the ugly.

When you're having a dinner conversation, remember a few etiquette rules. The first is to keep the conversation clean. In other words, no potty talk: farts, poo, and pee-pee should not be mentioned at the dinner table. This might make people lose their appetite. If you feel the need to tell a joke, make it a clean one. If you do need to use the bathroom, simply say, "Excuse me."

The second conversation rule at the dinner table is to talk and share, but also to be a good listener. Let other people talk and chime in, and listen to what they have to say. One person should never dominate the whole conversation. Avoid interrupting other people when they are talking, even if you are really excited about what you're trying to say. Dinnertime talk is about sharing and listening. If no one is really talking, you can always ask everyone how their days were.

- SPOTLIGHT ON -
MRS. BEETON

Isabella Mary Beeton (1836–1865) was an English journalist and editor who wrote the well-known book Mrs. Beeton's Book of Household Management. *After the publication of her popular book in 1861, Mrs. Beeton was known as the authority on Victorian home management and cooking. Her book is still in print and revered today, more than 150 years later. Mrs. Beeton died tragically at the age of 28, but her name reigns on as a legacy of domestic authority.*

What do you do on those days when it seems like there is nothing to talk about? Try playing this conversation-starter game. It will liven up your dinner table!

CONVERSATION STARTERS

Write down the following conversation starters on scraps of paper. Feel free to use these or to make up your own! Keep these scraps of paper folded up in a clean jar with a lid. During dinner, pull a few of these from the jar and have everyone share their answers to the questions.

What is your dream job?

When you are Mom and Dad's age, what do you see yourself doing?

If you could travel anywhere in the world, where would you go?

Would you rather live on the beach or in the mountains? Why?

If you could travel back in time, what time period would you visit? Why?

What's the scariest thing that has happened to you?

Share your most embarrassing story.

What makes you feel loved?

If you could have one superpower, what would it be?

What's one thing you could have done better today?

What's your favorite place in the home?

Say one nice thing about the person to your left.

What are the three most interesting things about you?

If you could trade places with your parents/kids today, what would you do differently?

What was the best part of your day?

Share how you think your parents met. Then have your parents tell you how they actually met.

What is your all-time favorite meal?

What is something you want to learn to do?

Do you believe in miracles? What is a miracle you'd like to see happen?

If you could have any animal in the world as a pet, what would you have and what would you name it?

What are the most important things your parents have taught you?

What's the best thing about our family?

What's your favorite family tradition?

What two things would you take with you to a desert island?

Name two things you like about yourself and one thing you'd like to change.

What would you do if you were a king or a queen?

Cleaning Up

After dinner is over, it's nice for the whole family to pitch in and help clean up. Here is a guide to getting the kitchen cleaned quickly. If the whole family works together, it's actually quite fun. Put some music on and the after-dinner cleanup will fly by. Which of these duties is your favorite to do?

DISHWASHING DUTY

Gather all of the plates at the dinner table. Scrape all of the leftover food onto one plate. Stack the rest of the plates and bring them to the sink full of soapy water. Deposit the leftover food collected on the one plate into the trash or compost. Add that dish to the sink. Add all of the leftover silverware and drinking glasses to the sink as well. Collect everything that needs to be washed. Now, put the dishes in the dishwasher, if you have one, or scrub and rinse them, and set them out to dry, if you are washing by hand.

TABLE DUTY

Once all of the dishes, silverware, and glasses have been collected, clear all other items off the table. Place any cloth napkins, place mats, or tablecloths in the laundry bin to be washed. If the place mats are not stained, they may be used again. Place any condiment or drink bottles back in the refrigerator. Now that you have a clear table, spray it with a cleaning solution and wipe it down. Push in all of the chairs and you are done!

COUNTERTOP DUTY

Clear off the counter by categories. First, look for everything that belongs in the refrigerator, and put those items away. Then look for all items that belong in the pantry and do the same. Look for all items to be thrown in the trash or recycling, like empty cans, packages, and used paper products. Then collect everything that needs to be washed, and bring that to the kitchen sink. Once your countertops are clear, spray them with a cleaning solution and wipe them down.

FLOOR DUTY

After every other job in the kitchen has been done, it's time for floor duty! Place chairs upside down with the legs up on top of the kitchen table. Get out the broom, and sweep all of the crumbs and dirt into a pile. Sweep the pile into a duster pan, and dump it in the garbage. Some evenings you can mop the floor, too, but it doesn't have to be done every night. Place the chairs back in their proper place, and that's floor duty!

- CONNOISSEUR KIDS ACTIVITY -

FAMILY TABLE MANNERS CHALLENGE

You've learned a lot of tips on how to have great manners at the dinner table. This week, involve your entire family. Each weekday, you will focus on one skill.

Monday: good posture
Tuesday: proper napkin use
Wednesday: using your silverware correctly
Thursday: trying a new food
Friday: improving your conversation skills

Every night, announce the subject that you will all be focusing on. This isn't just for you; it's for Mom and Dad, too! As you move on to each new day, don't lose the skills you practiced the day before. In other words, by Friday, when you are working on your conversation skills, you will also be sitting with good posture, placing your napkin in your lap, and using your silverware correctly. Soon these good table manners will just naturally radiate from you!

Mealtimes are some of the most special times of the day. They are a chance to bond with your family members, nourish your body, and relax and unwind. When everyone uses their best manners at the table, the experience is even more enjoyable. (Remember, the more you practice, the more naturally they will come to you, and soon, you won't think twice about doing them.)

3

TIDINESS

Parents, the goals of this chapter are to: 1. Learn how to be tidy;
2. Practice tidying on a daily basis; and 3. Actually enjoy tidying.

Most people aren't born tidy, so don't worry if you struggle in this area. Almost everyone has to learn how to be tidy. Being tidy is more important than you probably realize. It gives you good habits that you'll carry with you for the rest of your life! The first step to being tidy is to have a cheerful attitude about it.

Let's think back to a time in the not-so-distant past. When your parents asked you to clean your room, did you groan inwardly? Or did you spring to your feet with excitement to get the task done? I'm guessing you groaned! You would rather [insert anything here] than clean your room.

I'm going to let you in on a secret: you probably don't like to clean your room because you don't know how to do it! Sure, you know how to hang clothes, make your bed, and push a vacuum, but what about all those other troublesome things scattered across the floor? It's so daunting to figure out where everything goes. It seems to take forever! Once you learn the secret to cleaning your room, you will look at it as a fun challenge. You might even spring to your feet at the chance to tidy your room!

START WITH
A CHEERFUL
ATTITUDE

Sometimes we are called to be cheerful, but we just don't feel like it. Let's try an exercise that will probably make you laugh. Get comfortable on the sofa reading this book. Have your mom, or another family member, ask you to clean your room. Spring to your feet, and with the happiest and most cheerful attitude you've *ever* had, say, "Yes, ma'am (or sir)!" Then run to your room. Your parent might faint with joy! Try this exercise two or three times. There might be a lot of laughter, but when you respond with a joyful heart regularly, it really becomes a habit. Ready? Set? Go!

TIDYING YOUR ROOM

The best tip, other than having a cheerful attitude about cleaning your room, is to tidy by categories. Categories are things that have shared characteristics, in other words, things that are similar in nature. When you tackle one category at a time, you are able to clean your room in an efficient way. Selecting categories and actively putting them away is a fun challenge that stimulates your brain.

TIDY BY CATEGORIES EXERCISE

Take this book and travel to your room. Maybe your room is already tidy because you recently cleaned it, or maybe it's a disaster! Either way, you can still do this exercise. Have a look around and see if there are any objects lying out that don't belong where they are.

The following chart should help you categorize your belongings. On the left side of the chart, the categories are listed. Sample categories are: clothes, books, toys, papers, and craft supplies. On the right side of the chart is listed "Where it belongs." Here you will write where these things go. For example, for the category of clothes, you might write, "Dirty clothes go in the hamper, drawers, and closet." Where you put your clothes will depend on whether they are clean or dirty. It's OK to have more than one location listed in the "Where it belongs" column. There are a few empty spaces at the bottom of the chart. Feel free to fill them in with any categories you have that are not covered. Your exercise right now is to look around your room, find your categories, and list where they belong.

CATEGORY	WHERE IT BELONGS
Clothes	
Books	
Toys	
Papers	
Craft supplies	

Keeping your room nice and neat
Isn't so much of a difficult feat.
Clean by categories is what to do.
A cheerful attitude always helps, too!

Tidy Every Day?

Now that you know the secrets to keeping a tidy room (to tidy by categories with a cheerful heart), you should aim to keep your room tidy every day. This might seem like an impossible feat! But if you do a little work every day, your room can always be tidy. You can still have fun in your room by doing craft projects and building forts, but you can also easily tidy it up so your room is a clean slate for the next adventure you embark on.

The best thing you can do to maintain tidiness is to clean up right after every activity you do in your room. In other words, before moving on to a new activity, always put your old one away. This can seem so hard when you are excited to move on to the next thing, but when you tidy up after yourself regularly, you make life easier for yourself. Your room never gets to code-red disaster status!

Before you go to bed each night, look around your bedroom. If you didn't have a chance to tidy and your room is a disaster zone, take a few minutes to tidy it up.

A Place for Everything

When you're cleaning your room, do you ever encounter an object that you just don't know what to do with? Have you ever heard the expression "A place for everything and everything in its place"? Every single thing you have in your room, from the biggest thing to the smallest thing, should have a home or a "place." If you find over and over that you don't know where to put a certain thing, it's time to create a home for it. If you have many things that don't have homes, your temptation when tidying your room might be to shove everything under the bed. While that would certainly be easier, it won't solve the problem of where to permanently put your belongings. When every category has a home (for example, all papers in your desk, all markers in a bin box, and all books on the bookshelf), tidying up by category is so much easier.

> When tidying up your room,
> Everything deserves a home.
> Don't let that teddy bear wander,
> Don't let those Legos roam.
> Find a spot where they can live.
> Don't shove them under your bed.
> Next time you tidy up your room,
> You'll already be ahead!

A PLACE FOR EVERYTHING CHALLENGE

Now that you've become a connoisseur of giving a proper home to all of your belongings, try this fun challenge to test your newfound skills. Have a family member collect five random things from your room. For example, a pair of pajamas, a book, a toy, a marker, and a coloring book. Then you are going to do a relay race with only you doing the running! Have your family member hold the items at the door of your bedroom. With the timer ticking, take one item from your family member and put it away properly where it goes. When you are finished, you may run back and get the next item. See how fast you can put these objects away. Try to get your best time! Then you can trade and do the same game for the family member you played with.

DO WHAT YOU UNDO

Here's a tip that will help keep the mess in your house to a minimum. Always remember to do what you undo. Here are some examples: If you open a drawer, shut it. If you open a cabinet, close it. If you pull out a chair, push it in. If you open a door, close it behind you. If you pull out a toy, put it away. If you take something out of the refrigerator, put it back. If you get out the scissors, put them back when you're finished with them. Always do what you undo, and don't move on until you've done it.

MAKE IT FUN: SET A TIMER

Another secret to tidying up any space is to set a timer. You can use a sand timer, if you have one, or a digital kitchen timer. If you don't have a timer, you could always play two of your favorite songs. Start by setting the timer for 5 minutes. When you press "go" (or "play" if you're timing yourself by music), work furiously the entire time. You will be amazed at not only how quickly the time goes but also by how much you get done in that short period of time! Challenge yourself to see if you can beat the clock and finish before the timer goes off. If you have extra time, you can celebrate and dance, or you can keep going and do something extra (like polish your rock collection).

DIY Storage Crafts

No place to put your pencils? What about those little toys that just seem to be scattered everywhere? By recycling everyday household items, you can make nice-looking storage containers for all of your smaller belongings. Here are some ideas:

Cover an empty coffee canister with wrapping paper, and paint it with Mod Podge. After it dries, you have a great place to store your pens, pencils, and markers.

Cover a shoebox with an attractive fabric, and glue it into place. Do the same with the lid, if you need one. This can hold everything from stamps to Legos to card games.

Recycle a tea tin to store really tiny belongings, like beads.

SPOTLIGHT ON:
PAUL CÉZANNE

One of the most famous painters of still lifes was the French Post-impressionist painter Paul Cézanne (1839–1906). Even though Cézanne was also very accomplished at portraits and land-scapes, his still-life paintings remain some of the best known in art history. His painting Still Life with a Curtain (1895) *depicts a casual scene of fruit in bowls, with a pitcher and rumpled nap-kins before an ornate curtain. Check out a book on still life at the library to further your knowledge of this wonderful artistic style.*

DONATE WHAT YOU DON'T NEED

For this activity, you get to be the boss! Collect as many large trash bags as you have family members. If there are five people in your family, for example, you will grab five bags. Gather everyone together in your living room. Distribute one bag per family member. Instruct each person to fill their bag with items that they would like to donate to people who are less fortunate than you are. You will do this by bringing your filled bags to a local charity shop.

If any of your brothers or sisters don't want to part with their belongings, you can remind them that doing this will bring joy to others! Items to put in the bags could include clothing and shoes that no longer fit, toys that are no longer played with, and books that you have outgrown. Get out your trusty timer, and give everyone a set amount of time: usually 15 to 20 minutes should do the trick. Once everyone is clear on the rules, you can send them off. Remember, for this challenge, you're the boss!

STILL LIFE WITH MESSY AND CLEAN ROOM

Capture the before and after of your room tidying with this fun art activity. Do you know what a still life is? In the art world, a still life is usually a painting of inanimate objects, or things that don't move. The subjects are usually everyday objects, nothing fantastic: think the contents of a kitchen countertop or the vase of flowers in your dining room. Working on a still life is fun because you hone your drawing or painting skills when you try to depict the objects as realistically as possible.

Your still life is going to be your room, but with a twist. You are going to capture the before and after of your messy and tidy room. Choose a time when your room is messy and in need of tidying. Before you tidy up your room, break out your art supplies and sit down in a place where you have a view of your whole room. You can use anything you like: pencil and paper, pastels, markers, crayons, or even watercolors. I suggest you use a large piece of sketch paper.

Divide the paper in half with a line. On the left-hand side, draw your room when it looks messy. Capture everything you can: clothes that haven't been put away, toys scattered on the floor, the unmade bed. Everything. Then set the timer for 15 minutes and tidy up your room. Aim to make this your best attempt at tidying. Make your room look beautiful. When you are done, sit down in the same spot, and on the right side of the paper, draw your newly tidied room from the same viewpoint.

Have fun with this still-life activity, and hang up your masterpiece on the wall to always inspire you to keep your room like the right side of the picture, not the left.

When You Share Your Room

Now that you are a tidy connoisseur of your bedroom, you will always want to keep it tidy. But what do you do if you share your bedroom with your brother or sister? If you share your bedroom with your sibling, you are actually at an advantage, because when it comes to tidying, two people are better than one. You have an extra pair of hands to help tidy up your room!

Now, on the flip side of this, you also have an extra pair of hands to mess it up. Work together with your brother or sister to maintain a tidy space. Make sure your sibling knows the secret of cleaning by categories and making it fun by timing yourselves while you clean. This habit of keeping your room clean will become a fun part of your day.

TIDYING THE BATHROOM

Whether you have a bathroom all to yourself or you share one with your whole family, it's good to know how to keep it tidy. It's especially important to keep a bathroom tidy because bathrooms can be full of germs. Yikes! To prevent sickness, we should always try to keep the bathroom clean. Here are some Connoisseur Kids tips to keeping your bathroom tidy:

When you are about to take a bath, always put your dirty clothes in the clothes hamper, never on the floor.

When you're done with your bath, hang your towel back on the towel rack. Never (you guessed it!) place it on the floor.

When you brush your teeth, always place your toothbrush and toothpaste in their holder, not on the countertop (this helps keep your toothbrush clean, avoiding germs).

Keep your hairbrush and hair ties (if you use them) in the same spot. Avoid scattering them across the countertop.

Keep a spray bottle with a multipurpose cleaner (see recipe below to make your own!) and cleaning cloths under the sink, and try to wipe down the countertop when you notice it getting dirty.

If you accidentally splash water on the mirror, you can wipe it down with the spray and cloth.

Lavender Vinegar Spray

This lavender spray works well and smells wonderful!

Makes 1 cup [240 ml]

½ cup [120 ml] distilled white vinegar
½ cup [120 ml] water
20 or 40 drops lavender essential oil (optional)

Take an empty spray bottle (you can purchase one at the dollar store, or you can use a used spray bottle that is empty; just be sure to clean it out before using it). Fill it with the white vinegar and water. If you don't like the vinegar smell, you can add essential oils like lavender, lemon, or tea tree oil. You will need 20 to 40 drops of oil. Shake it up and you have an all-natural cleaner. Make sure you label the bottle. You will love to clean the bathroom mirror and countertops with this!

The Toilet, Floor, and Bathtub

I'm sure the title of this section has you shaking your head. The toilet? The floor? The bathtub? Aren't those only supposed to be cleaned by Mom and Dad? Not necessarily! If you want to go the extra mile and clean the bathroom all the way, here's how you do it.

TO CLEAN THE TOILET: You must first get over your heebie-jeebies. That's another way to say don't be too grossed out by cleaning the toilet. Ask for a pair of cleaning gloves. Then, spray the toilet with antibacterial spray or the vinegar-water solution you made. Spray it from the top of the toilet to the bottom, including the seat and under the lid. Then wipe the toilet down with paper towels in that same order, starting from the top of the toilet (don't forget the handle!), working your way down. Make sure you do the seat and under the lid last. Throw away the paper towels. Now get a toilet bowl cleaner and squirt it inside the bowl (this part is actually fun) and scrub the bowl with a toilet brush. Flush. Stand back and enjoy your handiwork!

TO CLEAN THE FLOOR: Lift everything off the floor, including bath mats. Move the dirty clothes hamper out of the bathroom if you need to. Now sweep or vacuum up all of the dust and particles. Then use the vinegar-water solution you made (or another cleaner) and spray the floor. With a mop, go over the areas you sprayed, and see how shiny your floor can be!

TO CLEAN THE BATHTUB: Grab a cup or so of baking soda and place it in your bathtub. Baking soda is great to clean with because it's natural and doesn't have any harsh chemicals. Spray the baking soda with your vinegar-water solution. This will make the baking soda fizz. With a wet sponge or cloth, rub down your bathtub in circular motions and watch all of the dirt and grime melt away. When you are done, wash it all down the drain with water. Voilà! A clean and sparkly bathtub!

KEEPING THE WHOLE HOUSE TIDY

Now that you are a connoisseur of keeping your own room and bathroom tidy, we are going to talk about the rest of the house. If everyone in the home kept their own bedroom and one other room in the house clean, think about how tidy the house would be on a daily basis. Mom and Dad would be so helped by this. Sit down with your family and implement the special room plan.

If there is a room in the house that you'd like to be responsible for, you can ask for that room. If you're having trouble deciding, however, or if two people want the same room, here's what you do: Write down all of the rooms in your home (except for bedrooms—each person is responsible for their own) and place them in a bowl. Each person can choose a paper from the bowl, and that is the room they are assigned to for the whole month.

It will be your job by the end of each day to make sure that room is tidy.

You can really get into this exercise and take pride in how you do "your room." Now you know tidying is easier when done by categories, so this daily challenge will be a breeze for you. If the living room is the room you chose, for example, your categories could be sofa, coffee and end tables, and floor. You can fluff the sofa pillows and arrange them nicely. Clear off anything that shouldn't be on the coffee table, like empty glasses or old newspapers. Pick up any toys on the floor and even run a vacuum over the rug, if necessary. Cleaning by categories in your special room will be not only challenging in a good way, but also fun! And think of how you will help your family by doing this. When the month is over, you get to choose a different room and work on perfecting that one.

Areas for Special Attention

Your Backpack:
Our rooms, bathrooms, and special rooms aren't the only places we should keep tidy. We should also keep our personal belongings tidy. Your school backpack, for example, can quickly get messy. Old papers, crumbs, water bottles, snacks, and pieces of trash can accumulate in your backpack. Every day, make sure that all food is taken out of your backpack. If you leave food in there for long periods of time, it can get moldy and smelly. Aim

to drink your entire water bottle so that it is empty at the end of every day. You can refresh it at home by cleaning the bottle and refilling it with water for the next day.

Once a week, do a deep clean of your backpack. Take everything out and discard all of the trash. Once you're sure that all items (including change) are out of the bag, hold the bag upside down over a trash bag so you can discard all of the crumbs and lint in your bag. Wipe the inside down with a damp cloth, dry it, and return your belongings to their place. Sharpen your pencils, if needed. Check to make sure you are not running low on hand sanitizer. Clean your backpack regularly, and you won't be lugging around a lot of unnecessary items with you each day at school.

Your Desk:
Along with your backpack, your desk can also get messy, fast. Whether this is your desk at school or at home, regularly go through it to tidy and disinfect. You are probably holding on to all sorts of things in your desk: old papers that you no longer need, half-finished art projects, broken crayons, and other bits and pieces. Each week, throw away everything that does not belong and that you no longer need. Sweep out any crumbs or small pieces of paper. Once a week, take a disinfecting wipe, or your homemade vinegar-water spray, and wipe down your desk to clear away any germs or bacteria.

The Backseat of the Car:
The car is another place that can get messy, quickly. You can help keep the car clean by being responsible for your seat area. If you

have any snacks that fall or drinks that spill in the car, wipe them up at your next opportunity. Whatever you bring into the car, such as toys or papers, should always come out. Avoid collecting things in the car. If you ever sip a drink in your seat, such as a smoothie, for example, always bring it out and throw it away when the car ride is over. You don't want to have the unpleasant experience of finding a moldy cup of liquid the next time you hop in for a ride. Always avoid putting your shoes on the seat in front of you because you might get it dirty, and then you'll have to look at a dirty seat while riding in the car. Keep your personal space in the car clean, and you will help your family travel in style.

Tidy While Traveling

When you are traveling, your tidiness skills travel with you. This starts by packing your suitcase neatly and efficiently. Make sure all bottles in your toiletries bag are fully closed, and zip up your bag before placing it into the suitcase. When you arrive at your destination, unpack your suitcase when you are shown your room. Place your neatly folded clothes in the dresser drawers, closet, or bureau provided. If you are not unpacking (if you are just staying overnight), keep your clothes neatly folded in your suitcase.

Always bring a "dirty clothes bag" in your suitcase when you travel. You could even use an empty pillowcase for this. Place all dirty clothes in this dirty clothes bag so that you do not sully your neatly folded clean clothes. When you are staying at someone's house, always keep your suitcase and clothes neat and out of the way. Never leave your clothes strewn across the floor or in the common areas of the house. Take your tidiness skills with you every time you travel.

PRACTICE TIDINESS HABITS

Practice your new tidiness habits starting today. Get excited about keeping a clean room and bathroom. Help your family tidy the house with a happy heart, and enjoy being an important part of making your home beautiful. Keep your personal belongings and spaces clean, like your backpack and your desk. Good habits of tidiness are formed when you are young. If you start these good habits now, they will follow you for the rest of your life. Well done, tidy connoisseur!

4

THINKING OF OTHERS

Parents, the goals of this chapter are to: 1. Learn selflessness;
2. Put thoughtfulness into action on a daily basis; and 3. Enjoy helping
and serving others.

In order to be a well-rounded Connoisseur Kid, we will work on our manners, tidiness, hygiene, and grooming, but we must not forget one of the most important parts of life: our relationship to other people, including how we treat them. Treating people well is a big part of good etiquette. All day long you will interact with other people: your family, your classmates, your teachers, your friends, your neighbors, your coaches, your teammates . . . the list goes on! We want to be known for treating others well through acts of kindness and selflessness. You can even inspire others to act the same way. Isn't that a neat thought?

It's normal human nature to want to put yourself first. We all have that urge! If there is a plate of cookies offered, you probably want to reach for the biggest one. When you put others before yourself, you offer someone else the biggest cookie and are happy with the one you get. It's a challenge, because it goes against what you really want! But there is fun in the challenge. Each day will bring you many instances where you can put others before yourself. Excitedly accept each one, and see what you can do for other people. The key, of course, is to do this with a happy heart.

PUTTING OTHERS BEFORE YOURSELF

Putting others before yourself often means that you are doing something you don't want to do, but you know you are helping the other person, so you do it. For example, after dinner, even though you want to play video games, you help your parents sweep the kitchen floor. You're putting their needs before your own wants. Here is a list of examples for putting others before yourself. There are two blanks on the following page. Feel free to add your own ideas that pertain to your life.

PUTTING OTHERS BEFORE YOURSELF

Offering the biggest cookie to someone else

Helping your brother or sister clean their room so they can go out to play sooner

Saying hello to the new person at school and asking if they want to sit with you at lunch

Helping Mom and Dad with the housework, even if it's not one of your assigned chores

Helping a sick family member by bringing them a glass of juice and a book

Picking up a friend if they fall down

Letting someone else have the seat that you wanted to sit in

Helping unload the groceries from the car

The idea is to think about how you can serve others. When most people think of a server, they think of a waiter or waitress at a restaurant. They are also called servers. It is their job to take your order, pour your drinks, and bring your food. They frequently check on you to see if you are OK and take your food away at the end of the meal. Basically, they're looking after you. This is how we want to be in our life. We want to serve others gladly. Can you imagine if your waiter served your table but slammed down your plates and complained the whole time he was doing his job? That would be very unpleasant for you. That's why when we serve others, we want to do it with a happy heart. Doing things for other people to make their lives better should make us feel happy. Your happiness will naturally shine through.

Can you think of a time when you served another person and how it made you feel? Write it down here:

SPORTSMANSHIP

Whether you play on a sports team or just occasionally play games with the neighborhood kids, good sportsmanship is a quality that everyone needs. If you play sports regularly, you have the opportunity to work on your sportsmanship regularly! What is sportsmanship? How would you define it?

Good sportsmanship is fair and generous treatment of others while you are playing a game. Here is a chart that shows good and bad sportsmanship. See what you can add to the chart.

GOOD SPORTSMANSHIP	BAD SPORTSMANSHIP
Accepting when the other team scores a goal; they won it fair and square . . .	Screaming to the ref that the other team's goal was not fair
Celebrating quickly when your team scores a point and then moving on to continue playing the game	Taunting the other team members and gloating about your team's point by doing a long, drawn-out dance in the sidelines
Checking on an injured member of the opposite team	Not helping someone when they're injured because they aren't on your team
Shaking the hand of the winning team and congratulating them when the game is finished	Kicking the ground and running off the field when you lose

Good sportsmanship applies not only when you're playing sports but also any time you play a game with others. When you play a game, it's fun to win, but that's not the whole point of playing. The point of playing games is to enjoy fellowship with other people. What's fellowship? It's a fun and friendly gathering of people. It's hanging out with family and friends, or even making new friends! The point of the game is to bond together and enjoy each other's company. If you ever feel yourself getting angry over the results of the game, just take a deep breath and remember why you're playing in the first place: not to win, but to enjoy the journey. If you win, that's just the cherry on the cake!

When you play a game,
It's not all about the win.
You want to start happy
And leave with a grin.
But that grin is not determined
By whether or not you won.
It's the natural thing that happens
Through true fellowship and fun.

Thoughtfulness

You can serve others not only by doing good deeds to help them out, but also by doing thoughtful things for them. Being a thoughtful person means you often think about others and what you can do for them. Picking a bouquet of flowers for your mother or sister, creating a card for someone who is going through a hard time, writing a letter to an elderly relative: these are all thoughtful acts that aren't necessary but would be very appreciated. They are little kind gestures that show you care.

- CONNOISSEUR KIDS ACTIVITY -

WRITE A THOUGHTFUL LETTER

Today you're going to write a letter to an elderly relative. Maybe it's your great-grandmother or an elderly uncle who lives alone. Break out the pencil and paper, and write your relative a nice, juicy letter. Tell them what you've been up to, what your favorite activities are, who your best friend is. Tell them your favorite color and subject in school. Ask them questions about their life. If you are able, arrange to visit them soon and let them know you're coming. If you like to draw, you can also include some of your artwork. If you have a recent picture of you and your family, send that, too. Seal up the letter, address and stamp the envelope, and walk it down to the mailbox. Your letter will brighten their day so much more than you even know!

Don't make this letter a onetime event. Schedule on your calendar once a month to write to your relative. Your regular correspondence will be something they look forward to. Your letters will be cherished, and your thoughtfulness will brighten their day.

How to Address an Envelope

When you address an envelope, your address goes in the top left-hand corner. The addressee's information goes in the center of the envelope. Capitalize all proper names, including street name, city, and state or province. The stamp goes in the top right corner of the envelope. Make sure you have enough postage. If your envelope is an odd shape, or if the contents of your letter are heavy, you may need more than one stamp. If you are sending your letter internationally, you will need more postage than if you send it nationally. Here is an example of a properly addressed envelope:

Jane Johnson
1234 Rose Street
Westerly, RI 12345

Mrs. Adelaide Johnson
2345 Fountain Place
Everville, OH 56789

THINKING OF OTHERS FIRST

It's very easy to go about your day thinking of yourself first: what you want and what you need. Thinking of others and how you can help them doesn't come as naturally. It's actually something that needs to be practiced. Why bother practicing this at all? When you think of yourself all the time, you become self-centered. It may sound strange, but when you think of others before yourself, you actually feel happier in the long run. Serving and helping others is a wonderful feeling and makes the world a better place to live in.

Selfish vs. Unselfish

Ah, the word *selfish*. We've all heard it before. Maybe someone has accused you of being selfish. Or maybe you've thought other people have acted selfishly. Being selfish is something that we have all been guilty of at one point or another. Can you guess the one word that is associated with being selfish?

It's *me. Me! Me! Me!* If you've ever thought someone was being selfish, you probably noticed that they were only thinking of themself and didn't care about the feelings of others. Someone refuses to share a toy with you, or doesn't give you a turn in a game. Someone is "hogging" something and not letting you use it. Someone took the last slice of cake and didn't think to share it. When people are selfish, it can enrage us, which is why it's important that we make sure we are not being selfish.

The antidote (or solution) to selfishness is thoughtfulness. Thoughtfulness and serving others, as we have already experienced, doesn't come naturally and can often be the hardest choice to make. It's easier just to be selfish and fulfill our own wants first. But as Connoisseur Kids, we are going to regularly practice the selfless acts of thoughtfulness and serving others so that they do become the natural course of action.

If there is ever a time where you know you're being selfish—let's say you don't want your brother to play with a toy—it's never too late to reverse your actions and share. You can change your mind so easily about this. You can douse the flames of the situation by immediately ending the selfish behavior and choosing to share and serve others. Just sit back and watch the benefits from this scenario! It might be annoying at first. After all, you wanted that toy! But when you see the joy that you can bring others and experience the joy of sharing your toy and playing with your brother, you know that, just like with games, the fun is in the journey, not the outcome.

When I am being selfish,
It's all about me, me, me!
What I want and what I need
Is of the utmost, can't you see?
But I see the sadness it causes
And that my actions are not that nice.
I pause for a moment and realize
Being selfish is a vice.

- CONNOISSEUR KIDS TIP -

BE SELFLESS, NOT SELFISH

We want to be selfless, not selfish. Being selfless is being kind and putting others before yourself. Being selfish is only thinking about yourself and always putting yourself first. The character trait of selflessness is rare and shines like a valuable gem. Work on being selfless, and you will stand out for your kindness, inspiring others to do the same.

REFLECT ON SHARING

Write about a time that you shared during the week and how it made you feel. Draw a picture showing what happened.

_____

_____

_____

_____

_____

_____

Look at the Other Person's Perspective

Whenever you get into a disagreement with someone, try to look at things from their perspective. Have you ever heard the expression "Put yourself in my shoes"? What does that mean? It doesn't mean that you actually wear someone else's shoes; it means that you are looking at life from that person's point of view. If you meet someone who is always grumpy, you might be annoyed by their grumpiness. You might think, "What's wrong with him, anyway?" If you look at life through the other person's perspective, you might see why he is grumpy. Maybe he has a painful disability, or maybe he is sad because he got a bad grade on a test or is being bullied. Before we get annoyed and judge people, we should look at life from their perspective and have compassion for them.

Volunteer

A great way to put others before yourself and be of service is to volunteer. *Volunteer* means to give your time for free to help other people. There are so many things you can volunteer for. You could help clean the beach. You could help feed the homeless in a soup kitchen. You could donate your time at an animal shelter. You could spend time with children who have to be in the hospital for a long period of time. You could read to the elderly in an assisted living home. There are so many things you can do! Commit to volunteering as a family, and make it a regular and meaningful experience. You will see how good it feels to help others by donating your time.

Use Kind Words

The words we say are very important. Have you ever said something that you later regretted? You probably felt awful after saying it. Maybe you said something mean to a brother or sister, or maybe you yelled at your mom. Once words are said, they can never be unsaid. Of course, you can apologize for speaking unkindly, but the other person will remember the harsh words for a long time. That's why Connoisseur Kids never make fun of other people. They never call people names, and they don't insult others. They have compassion for people. If you see someone being bullied, you can comfort that person and tell him or her you think they're great. Counteract mean words with kind words. It's the Connoisseur Kid thing to do.

Sometimes mean words are said to someone's face and sometimes they are said behind their back. As you aim to always speak kind words, what should you do if you are with people who are talking badly about someone else when they are not there? This is called *gossip*. Gossip is speaking negatively about people when they are not there to defend themselves. Gossip is very hurtful. We just explored how to look at life through another person's perspective, and it's great to do that here, too. How would you feel if you were the one everyone was gossiping about? It would be very hurtful, and you would not like it. If other people are gossiping, you can excuse yourself and leave the conversation. Do this with confidence, knowing that you are doing the right thing.

Forgive

Forgiveness is a powerful tool and, believe it or not, forgiving is putting others before yourself. When someone has done you wrong, by saying mean words, pushing you, or not sharing with you, you can forgive them. Forgiveness is not easy to do, especially if the other person hasn't even said, "I'm sorry"! But we must forgive. When we forgive others, we let go of our anger and can move on with life. If we refuse to forgive, we hold on to the anger, and that is not healthy. You have to let it go eventually, so you might as well do it right away. When someone has wronged you, forgive them and move on. Connoisseur Kids embrace forgiveness.

Forgive one another.
It's the right thing to do.
It isn't always the easiest choice,
Especially when you're mad, too!
But forgiveness eases the problem,
And you will definitely calm down.
The next time someone wrongs you,
Forgive them to erase your frown.

CARING FOR
A PET

D o you have any pets in your home—a dog, cat, bird, fish, or all of the above? You can learn many lessons in responsibility and service by taking care of your pet. It might already be your chore to feed the dog, but you can take it a step further by giving the dog exercise every day. Take your dog on a walk or throw the ball for him or her. Make sure your dog's water is always fresh, and be the one to give your dog a bath. By taking care of your pet, you are learning so many valuable life lessons.

No matter what kind of pet you have, there is always maintenance and care that is needed. Food, water, exercise, and clean bedding are required for many pets. For birds and fish, it's more about keeping their cages and aquariums clean. Put your pet responsibilities on a calendar and schedule when you are going to do them. For example, every other Friday, you could clean the fish tank. Caring for your pet gives you great nurturing skills that will last a lifetime. After all, we can be of service not only to people, but to animals, too!

GIVING AND RECEIVING GIFTS

Gift giving is one of the most thoughtful acts we can do. There is also thought behind how you receive gifts. When you give a gift to someone else, you are showing them gratitude. Always give a gift without expecting one in return. Giving should be a joyful act. If you are able to wrap your gift, make it look special. You don't need fancy or expensive wrapping paper for this. You could even use things you already have in your home.

How to Wrap a Gift

Before we get fancy with wrapping paper, let's learn how to wrap a gift properly.

1. Measure the correct amount of paper you will use by placing the gift upside down on the paper. Bring the end of the paper up to see how much you'll need to secure it and cover the gift. Once you've measured your paper, you may cut it.

2. Secure one side of the paper to the back of your present with tape.

3. Fold the edge of the other side of paper about ½ inch [12 mm] so that when you bring it up to meet the other seam, the folded edge looks straight and neat. Secure with tape.

4. Now fold the paper on the short sides of the present. Starting on one end, fold the top flap of paper on each side down onto the present. This will create a triangular shape. Now fold the triangle up to meet the taped seam you created in steps 2 and 3. Repeat on the other side.

5. Add a ribbon, bow, sticker, or other decorations.

HOMEMADE WRAPPING PAPER

Did you know one of the best items you can use for wrapping paper is actually a brown paper bag? It may not seem very special, but you can transform brown paper into beautiful gift wrap. You could also use brown shipping paper. This can be bought in bulk, and it lasts a long time. Now that you are a connoisseur at gift wrapping, let's explore the different ways you can use brown paper to wrap and decorate your gift.

Brown paper with elegant ribbon and flowers. Wrap your gift with brown paper. Secure with tape. Choose a ribbon. Any color will work. You could also use a natural ribbon, like twine. You might have some in the kitchen. Wrap the ribbon around the center of your gift in both directions, then tie with a bow at the top. Pick one or two small flowers from your garden and place the stems in the knot of the ribbon to secure. Lavender also works really well here and provides a nice scent.

Custom-decorated brown paper. Measure the amount of paper you will need to wrap your present. Cut. Before wrapping your present, decorate the paper with stamps or markers. Once your colorful paper is ready, wrap the present as usual, and tie with a ribbon.

Potato stamp paper. If you don't own any stamps, you can create your own with something you probably already have in your pantry: a potato! Cut a potato in half and press a small cookie cutter of your choice into the potato. Keep the cookie cutter there and, with the help of an adult, take a knife and cut a thick slice around the edge of the cookie cutter. This will allow the shape to stand out. Remove the cookie cutter. Apply paint to the raised stamp part of the potato with a paintbrush or by dipping your potato in a thin layer of paint. Stamp the potato onto your brown paper and allow it to dry before wrapping. Metallic paints, such as gold and silver, look wonderful, but any color will do.

Thank You, I Think?

You know the joy of giving gifts and you even know how to present a beautifully wrapped gift with items you already have at home. Receiving gifts is equally fun. It's so exciting to get a gift! The excitement of taking off the wrapping paper and revealing what's inside is thrilling. But what do you do if you don't like the gift you receive?

Before you react negatively, remember the purpose of gift giving: to show appreciation for the other person. Remember that someone is showing appreciation for you! That is the biggest gift. The gift itself is secondary to that. Always be grateful for any gift, and always say, "thank you." If you are disappointed, keep it to yourself, and remind yourself to be gracious and grateful.

When you open up a gift
And it's something you don't like,
Never say, "What on earth? What is this?
I wanted a bike!"
Instead, be grateful for the gift
That has so graciously been given to you.
Say "thank you," smile, and feel good knowing
That someone appreciates you, too.

BEING A
GOOD GUEST

When you are a guest in someone's home, whether you are spending the night or just there for the afternoon, you should be on your best Connoisseur Kids behavior. Being extra thoughtful about your actions will express gratitude and respect for your hosts. They are kindly thinking of you by inviting you to their home, and your beautiful behavior and manners will show you are thinking of them, too.

Have you ever heard the Spanish expression *Mi casa es su casa*? This means "My house is your house." Your hosts might say that to you to make you feel at home. While that is a nice invitation from your hosts, be cautious. There are certain things that we do in our own homes that we shouldn't do at our host's house, even if they are family. For example, in your home, you might enjoy making a pillow fort out of the cushions on your sofa. Isn't it fun to build forts in the living room? While your family may be used to it, your hosts may be horrified to walk into their living room and find all of the sofa cushions in an elaborate pile on the floor! This is an extreme example, but it illustrates the point that at other people's houses, we shouldn't just do what we naturally do in our own home.

Follow this chart with dos and don'ts to help you be an exemplary guest.

THE CONNOISSEUR KIDS GUIDE TO BEING A GOOD GUEST

Never run inside the house. Always walk.

Always put away whatever you take out.

Keep the common areas neat. If you play with toys in the living room, put them away when you're done.

Always ask if there is anything you can do to help, especially at mealtimes.

Keep the guest room tidy by making the bed and keeping your clothes neatly put away.

Never leave dirty clothes on the floor; always store them in your dirty clothes bag (an empty pillowcase works well for this).

Always wipe your shoes before entering the house. Or take your shoes off upon entering.

Never jump on the furniture or beds.

Always ask before getting something to eat from the refrigerator or pantry.

Thank your hosts with a thank-you card or note at the end of your stay.

BEING A
GOOD HOST

We know what it takes to be a good guest, but what does it take to be a good host or hostess? Hospitality is the friendly entertaining of guests. When you invite people over to your home, you are acting out of thoughtfulness. As our lives get busier with school, chores, and extracurricular activities, most of us have very little time to entertain friends. Maybe you have a playdate at your house once in a while. But what about opening your home for an afternoon and inviting a family over for lunch or tea?

NEIGHBORHOOD HOSPITALITY CHALLENGE

Get to know your neighbors better by inviting them over for a meal. It doesn't have to be anything fancy. You could even serve tea and cake. Simple!

ENTERTAINING CHECKLIST

Here is a list of things to do before your guests come over. These are all things your parents would normally do. Now that you're in the know, you can help them prepare for guests!

Clean the bathroom that guests will be using. Wipe down all countertops. Make sure there is plenty of toilet paper and that the toilet is clean. Wipe the mirrors and provide a fresh hand towel. A single cut flower in a vase by the sink also makes a nice touch.

Straighten up all of the rooms that guests will be seeing: the living room, kitchen, and dining room (if applicable). Fix the pillows on the sofa and fold the throw blankets. Quickly dust the surfaces with an old sock. Make sure all of the curtains are open to allow light to pour in. Open up the windows to keep the room fresh.

If the kitchen is a mess from cooking for the party, tidy by categories as best you can. Throw all trash away, fill the sink with soapy water, and place all dirty dishes and cooking utensils in the sink. Put all food back in the refrigerator and pantry. Wipe surfaces clean. Take anything out of the kitchen that doesn't belong there (such as a hairbrush, toys, books, etc.).

Put music on low. You get to choose!

Set the table if you're having a meal. (Refer to the table setting guide in the Table Manners chapter.) Or lay everything out for tea.

Now just relax and enjoy having your company over. Don't worry if something goes wrong. Your guests probably won't even notice! They'll just be grateful to be there.

Afternoon Tea Recipes

Afternoon tea is the easiest way to entertain guests. You can make some finger sandwiches, cookies, and cakes, and lay everything out with a pot of tea; your guests will be delighted. Here are some recipes that are easy to make, yet taste good and look fancy.

CUCUMBER SANDWICH

Take two slices of bread. Cover both pieces with a thin layer of spreadable herbed cheese. Place thinly sliced and peeled cucumbers on one piece of bread. Cover with the other piece of bread. Cut off the crusts, and slice in half diagonally to form two triangle shapes.

SALMON SANDWICH

Lay out a small amount of smoked salmon on a plate or cutting board. Squeeze a small amount of lemon juice over the salmon, and shake pepper on top. Spread the herbed cheese on one slice of bread. Place the seasoned salmon on top, and cover it with another piece of bread spread with the herbed cheese. Cut off the crusts, and slice into triangles.

PB&J SANDWICH

For a crowd favorite, provide peanut butter and jelly sandwiches. Spread the peanut butter on one slice of bread and the jelly on the other slice. Press the pieces together. It's fun to cut these sandwiches into shapes with a cookie cutter to make them different from the other sandwiches: you could do a star, heart, circle, or animal shape.

TUNA SANDWICH

In a small bowl, combine one 5-ounce [140-g] can of tuna (drained of its liquid), 1 tablespoon of mayonnaise, and finely chopped olives to taste. Spread on one piece of bread. Place a folded lettuce leaf on top. Place the other slice of bread on top, cut off the crusts, and slice into triangles or rectangles.

VEGGIE SANDWICH

Spread herbed cheese or cream cheese thinly on two slices of bread. Place thinly sliced vegetables on top of one of the pieces of bread: you could use tomatoes, lettuce, cucumbers, red onions, or any other vegetables you love. Add salt to taste. Place the other piece of bread on top, cut off the crusts, and slice into triangles.

EGG SALAD SANDWICH

Place eight eggs in a pot. Cover them with cold water and place on the stove over medium to high heat. Once the water starts boiling, set the timer for 8 to 10 minutes. After the timer goes off, carefully remove the eggs from the boiling water (you will need the assistance of an adult for this). Set the eggs aside to cool. If you want to cool them faster, place them in a bowl of ice water. When the eggs are cool, peel them, discard the shell, and place them in a medium-size bowl. Add ½ cup [120 g] mayonnaise, ¼ teaspoon paprika, and salt and pepper. Mash the eggs and other ingredients together with a fork or potato masher. Place the egg salad on sliced bread to form sandwiches. Cut off the crusts and cut into triangles or rectangles.

CREAM CHEESE AND JELLY SANDWICH

Spread cream cheese on one slice of bread and your favorite jam or jelly on the other slice of bread. Press the slices together and cut into fun shapes with a cookie cutter.

For the fanciest tea party, you can make all of the sandwiches, but for most smaller parties you can pick two or three to make. Once you make your sandwiches, display them on a platter, and cover with plastic wrap to keep them fresh. You could also put them on a tiered cake stand. Just make sure they are covered so they aren't stale by the time your guests arrive. Serve with hot tea, iced tea, or lemonade. What a fun and easy way to entertain friends!

Homemade Lemonade

*This lemonade is wonderful on a hot summer day.
Serve over ice!*

Makes 10 cups [2.4 L]

1¾ cups [350 g] sugar
8 cups [2 L] water
1½ cups [360 ml] lemon juice (seeds removed)

In a saucepan, cook the sugar and 1 cup [240 ml] of the water over medium heat until the sugar is dissolved. This will make a simple syrup for your lemonade. Once this cools, in a large pitcher, combine the simple syrup, remaining 7 cups [2 L] water, and the lemon juice. Stir and enjoy! For a variation, add crushed strawberries or blackberries for a refreshing berry lemonade.

WHEN NO ONE IS LOOKING

"Integrity is doing the right thing when you don't have to—when no one else is looking..."
—Charles Marshall

This chapter is all about relating to other people and putting the needs of others before yourself. We can do that in so many ways: by being kind, by being thoughtful, by forgiving others, by inviting them to our home, and so much more. But what about when no one is around? True integrity is often defined as doing the right thing when no one is looking. We should never do something only because we want to impress other people or get a reward from our parents. We should always act from the kindness of our own heart because it's the right thing to do. Never ask, "What can I get out of this situation?" but rather, "How can I be of service here?" A true test is how you act in situations when no one is looking. Do you do the right thing?

Do the right thing.
Not for a reward,
Not for recognition
Or so you can keep score.
But always just do
The next right thing,
And be content with
The joy your actions bring.

PUT OTHERS FIRST

Your assignment is to think of others and put them before yourself. Practice as many times as you can in as many different scenarios as you can. Start with your immediate family. See what happens and what changes. Notice your struggles and enjoy the triumphs. Work toward extending your helpfulness to others as well, and finish off with inviting friends over for a meal or tea. Serve others, be thoughtful, be a true Connoisseur Kid.

5

HYGIENE & GROOMING

Parents, the goals in this chapter are to: 1. Learn about proper hygiene and grooming; 2. Practice good hygiene on a daily basis; and 3. Enjoy taking care of the body through good hygiene and grooming.

Hygiene (pronounced hi-jean), or how we take care of our bodies to keep ourselves clean and healthy, is an important part of life for everyone. Good hygiene not only helps us look neat, but it keeps us healthy, too. In this section, we will talk about our skin, hair, nails, teeth, and even clothing. Our aim as Connoisseur Kids is to always look neat and presentable. If you practice now as a child, it will come naturally to you as an adult. Your body is an awesome thing, and by practicing good hygiene and keeping yourself well groomed, you are taking care of your body as best you can.

TAKING CARE OF YOUR SKIN

Did you know that the skin is your body's largest organ? In order to keep it healthy, we have to keep it clean. By bathing or showering regularly and washing your skin with a mild soap, you are keeping the pores of your skin clean and able to properly function. Bathe or shower in warm water and use a washcloth lathered up with a mild soap to wash off. Don't forget those hard-to-reach places like your back and the bottoms of your feet. Scrub gently and rinse thoroughly. After you bathe or shower, apply a body lotion so that your skin doesn't get dry and flaky. Pay close attention to your elbows, knees, hands, and the soles of your feet. These areas tend to get dry skin easily.

If you take a bath in the evening, wash your face in the morning before you start your day. Look closely at your face in the mirror to make sure you don't have any crust in the corners of your eyes, which could have formed when you were asleep. You can take the crust out gently with a cotton swab or the tip of a wet washcloth.

If you plan on being out in the sun for a long period of time, apply sunblock to any exposed skin, especially your face. Sun-block protects against the damaging rays of the sun and prevents your skin from burning. It can also prevent you from getting wrinkles and even skin cancer later. Apply a sunblock that has an SPF of 30 or 45. *SPF* stands for "sun protection factor."

Other ways to take care of your skin are by eating fruits and vegetables and drinking lots of water. Drinking the right amount of water helps rid your skin of toxins and even makes it appear to glow. How much water should you drink? Follow this chart to find out.

AGE	RECOMMENDED 8-OUNCE [240-ML] GLASSES OF WATER PER DAY
5-8 years old	7 glasses of water [1.7 L]
9-12 years old	8 to 10 glasses of water [2 to 2.4 L]
13+ years old	10 glasses of water [2.4 L]

Speaking of washing up, remember this golden hygiene rule: when you use the bathroom, *always wash your hands*. To effectively wash your hands, roll up your sleeves. Wet your hands under the running water, and then rub soap into your hands for a few seconds to build up a lather. Next, rub your hands together under warm running water for about 20 seconds. You can count to 20 or sing the alphabet song once to count. Dry your hands with the hand towel. If the hand towel gets wet or dirty, you can change it out for a clean one. Sometimes you might feel like you don't need to wash your hands because they are not dirty, but always wash your hands every time you use the bathroom. Germs are so small that you can't see them, and it's better to be safe than sorry.

> When you use the bathroom,
> Wash your hands of all those germs.
> Not only if you've been digging
> In the yard and playing with worms,
> But every time you're in there,
> Even if you think you don't need to!
> Wash your hands with warm water and soap,
> And dry them when you're through.

Other than washing your hands every time you use the bathroom, there are a few other occasions in which you should always wash your hands: before eating, when you first get home from any outing, and when you know your hands are just plain dirty. You never know what sort of germs you pick up in the world, so always wash your hands as soon as you get home. If your skin gets dry after you wash your hands, apply a hand cream or lotion to them. Washing your hands regularly will protect you from getting sick.

TAKING CARE OF
YOUR TEETH

D id you know that over 300 types of bacteria make up dental plaque? Brushing your teeth at least twice a day, morning and evening, is the way to go to maintain healthy teeth. When you are brushing, don't rush! Take your time and make sure your toothbrush goes over every tooth you have, front and back. Brush in soft, circular motions over your teeth.

Have you ever been through a drive-through car wash? Those giant scrubbing machines go thoroughly over every inch of the car. Imagine that's what you're doing with your teeth! Spit regularly, and rinse your toothbrush with water before the final few go-rounds.

Every night, and any time during the day when you have food stuck in your teeth, you should use dental floss. Take the floss and go between each and every tooth. It might tickle and feel a bit funny, but you're cleaning in between those cracks. When food gets stored between your teeth, cavities can form. Floss every single evening, even if you think you don't need to, to keep your teeth in top shape. You can floss before or after you brush your teeth. It's up to you!

Round out your brushing and flossing routine with a rinse of mouthwash. Swish a small amount of mouthwash around in your mouth for at least 20 seconds. Be careful not to swallow it! Then spit it back into the sink. Rinse the sink with water so that the basin isn't stained from your tooth-cleaning extravaganza. Keep up this routine, and the dentist will be so pleased when you visit with your healthy mouth of teeth.

The following chart shares the best and worst foods for your teeth. Many of the foods on the "worst" list are there because they stick to your teeth in between the cracks, or cover your teeth with sugar or acids, which can cause cavities. If you enjoy any of the foods on the "worst" list, try to brush and floss shortly after eating them.

THE BEST FOODS AND DRINKS FOR YOUR TEETH	THE WORST FOODS AND DRINKS FOR YOUR TEETH
Water	Sodas and sports drinks
Crunchy fruits and vegetables	Caramels and taffy candy
Dairy products like milk, cheese, and non-sugary yogurt	White bread
Leafy greens	Potato chips
Eggs	French fries
Fish	Sticky granola bars
Beans	Candy
Whole grains	Dried fruits
Chicken and beef	Acidic juices (drink them with a straw instead)
Nuts	Gummy fruit snacks
Tofu	Cookies and crackers

Always keep your tooth-brushing area neat in your bathroom. Place your toothbrush back in its holder after brushing. Avoid leaving it on the counter because it could pick up germs. Only use your own toothbrush, and never share with your siblings. Try to get toothbrushes that look different so you don't mix them up, or write your name on the handle. Keep your dental floss in a container as well, and place your mouthwash and rinse cups neatly against the mirror on your countertop. Take pride in caring for your pearly whites, and your dedication will pay off with always having healthy teeth.

Fun Dental Facts*

Tooth enamel (the hard, outer surface of your teeth) is the hardest substance in the human body.

Just like fingerprints, tooth prints are unique to each person. No two teeth are exactly the same shape and size. Even your baby teeth are unique!

Over the course of their lifetime, the average American spends the equivalent of 38.5 days brushing their teeth.

Humans only have two sets of teeth in their lifetime: baby teeth and permanent adult teeth.

Humans have four different kinds of teeth to help us cut, grind, and tear food: incisors, canine, premolars, and molars.

The first toothbrushes our early ancestors used were twigs with frayed ends. Ouch!

Scientists can tell a lot from people's teeth. Our teeth can reveal how old we are, what we eat and drink, and even where we live on earth.

* Information from: 123 Dentist; "10 Fun Facts about Teeth," www.123dentist.com/10-fun-facts-about-teeth; Children's Dental Village, "Interesting Facts about Teeth and Dentistry," www.childrensdentalvillage.net; and Mouth Healthy, "10 Things You Didn't Know about Your Toothbrush," www.mouthhealthy.org.

USING THE
BATHROOM

Let's talk about using the bathroom, something else that we all have to do! The big picture here is that we want to go to the bathroom as soon as our bodies tell us we need to. Don't wait, even if you're having the most fun of your life, or you might have a potty accident. It's happened to everyone at one point in life, and it can be embarrassing! So when your body is telling you to go to the bathroom . . . go!

While we are in the bathroom, we want to keep ourselves as germ-free as possible, and we want to keep the space neat for the other people who use it. Boys, we want to aim into the toilet accurately so we don't get any urine on the seat or floor. If you do miss the spot, clean it up after you're finished with a disposable wipe. Don't forget to wipe and flush the toilet and then wash your hands.

After you've gone potty,
Don't forget to flush,
Even if you're busy,
Especially if you're in a rush.
After you use the potty,
You want to hear that gush.
Don't leave a surprise for the next person.
Don't forget to flush!

When you are using a public restroom, choose a stall that looks as clean as possible. If you walk into one and it looks messy, try to find one that is cleaner. If you have to sit down on the toilet, always use the seat cover provided in the stall. Because it's a public restroom, lots of different bottoms have sat on that toilet, and the sheet protector protects you from other people's germs. Flush when you're through, wash your hands with soap and water, and dry with paper towels or the air dryer. Washing your hands after using the public restroom is even more important because of all of the extra germs in there.

SPOTLIGHT ON:

LOUIS PASTEUR

Louis Pasteur (1822–1895) was a French scientist who was famous for his groundbreaking discoveries in vaccinations, microbial fermentation, and pasteurization. He saved countless lives by creating the first vaccines for anthrax and rabies. He most famously developed the system to treat milk that prevents bacterial contamination. We call this process pasteurization, after his last name.

HYGIENE FOR COLDS

Have you ever been around someone who sneezed and forgot to cover their mouth? Chances are, you got sprayed by their sneeze! We know that germs travel in sneezes, so always sneeze into your arm, specifically the inside of the elbow, where your arm curves. Why here and not in your hands? When you sneeze into your hands, the germs stay on your hands. Then you spread the germs to everything you touch. You might touch door handles, phones, and even shake someone else's hand. Your germs could transfer to all of these places. But when you sneeze into your arm, you prevent the germs from spreading.

If you have a runny nose, always blow and wipe with a tissue. Discard the tissue in the trash after each use. This also helps prevent the spreading of germs. Always wash your hands after blowing your nose. If you're having trouble breathing because of a stuffed nose, you can use a few drops of saline spray in each nostril to help clear it. If the skin on your nose gets sore from wiping it so much, rub a small amount of petroleum jelly on the sore areas to soothe the skin.

CLEANING YOUR NAILS

When you're old enough to use nail clippers on your own, you can take care of trimming your nails whenever you like. We should avoid having long nails because they can tear easily and get in the way of everyday life. It's harder to dig, type, and play sports when your nails are long. Long nails also trap dirt underneath them, so keeping them short and neat is important.

The key to cutting your nails without getting any jagged edges is to cut on the right side of the nail, then on the left, and finally finish in the middle. Always leave a little bit of white on your nail; try not to cut them too short or they might hurt. If your nail is still sharp or jagged, you can run a nail file over it until it's smooth.

If you have a hangnail, or a piece of skin that is sticking out on the side of your nail, use the clippers to go to the bottom of it and clip it off. If you have dirt underneath your nails, you will have to use a separate instrument to get the dirt out. You can use a wooden nail stick or a metal nail cleaner. Start on one side under the fingernail and drag the stick all the way to the other side, picking up all of the dirt along the way. If you have dirt in the cuticles of your nails (the cuticles are the little ridges where your nail ends and your skin begins), you can use a nailbrush and scrub your hands under warm, soapy water. A great idea is to keep a nailbrush in your bathtub so you can scrub your nails every night.

The day can host a number of things:
Digging, piano, writing, and swings!
Let's keep our nails short and sweet.
Clean underneath them so they stay neat.
Whether you're a girl or a boy,
A king or a queen,
It's a good idea to keep your nails clean.

TAKING CARE
OF YOUR HAIR

Keeping your hair neat and clean is the next part of hygiene we will discuss. If you are a kid with short hair, this part will be a breeze for you! Just wash your hair regularly. Brush it in the morning and style it how you like it. Some people like to use gel to keep their hair in place.

If you have longer hair, you probably know all about the following word: tangles! No one likes to have tangles. Tangles make hair brushing painful. But you don't need to have tangles! You can avoid them by following a few simple steps on a daily basis.

When you wash your hair, brush through your tangles with a wet brush, or a brush specifically designed to tackle tangles. Brush your hair by sections, starting at the bottom of the hair, working your way up. By the time you get to the top of your head, your brush will glide smoothly down your hair because you freed up all of the tangles below.

To maintain a tangle-free head of hair out of the shower, brush it regularly, especially right before you go to sleep. If you have very curly hair, you might not be able to brush it as much, or you will flatten the curls.

DIY Hair Gel

Try making your own hair gel. This is fun and easy to do!

Makes 1 cup [240 ml]

½ to 1 teaspoon unflavored gelatin
1 cup [240 ml] warm water
Essential oil (optional)

Dissolve the gelatin in the warm water and mix thoroughly. Note that 1 teaspoon of gelatin will give your hair a strong hold, and ½ teaspoon will give a light hold. You can choose what you'd like. Let this sit in the refrigerator and cool for at least 3 hours, or until it has set. Add a few drops of essential oil after the gel has set, if you like. Chamomile, lavender, sandalwood, or peppermint work nicely and have a pleasant scent. You can funnel the gel into a labeled squeeze bottle to make it easier to apply. The gel will last 1 to 2 weeks. Store in the fridge to prolong the shelf life of the gel.

Many tangles are formed at night while you are sleeping and rubbing your head against the pillow. To avoid forming tangles at night, you can braid your hair, if possible, with one or two braids. When you wake up, you can take the braids out and brush through your hair again. Not only will you have the bonus of tangle-free hair, but your hair will also have a nice wave to it after sleeping in braids all night.

Have you ever noticed the buildup of hair on your hairbrush? With all of the hair brushing going on, you will need to keep your hairbrush clean. Clean it once a week by pulling out all of the old hair stuck between the bristles. If there is residue on the brush from hair products you use, such as gel, you can wash the brush under running water with a dab of shampoo. Let the brush dry completely. You can put it out in the sun to speed the process. Look after your hairbrush by cleaning it regularly and always keeping it in the same place.

How to Avoid Lice

Chances are, you've had lice once or you have known someone who has had lice. Having lice is never any fun. What are lice? They are tiny parasites that attach themselves to human hair to feed on human blood. Yuck! If you've ever had lice, you know how itchy your head can get. Don't worry. Getting lice is very common and doesn't mean you are dirty or that anything is wrong with you. If you get lice, there are many at-home treatments your parents can do to get rid of them. You can even go to lice removal salons to get rid of the pesky things. Once you discover someone has lice in your family, it's important to wash everything that has come in contact with that person's hair. All bedding, blankets, pillow covers, clothes, and hats should be thoroughly washed. Even car headrests should be wiped down with a disinfectant wipe. Floors and upholstery will need to be thoroughly vacuumed. All hairbrushes and combs will need to be washed with shampoo and left to dry in the sun.

Practice these prevention tips to save you from a bad lice experience.

Don't share items that touch the head of other people, like hairbrushes, hats, pillows, combs, or towels.

Avoid touching your head to someone else's head. The lice can easily jump from one head to another.

Use essential oils to deter lice. Lavender, eucalyptus, rosemary, peppermint, and tea tree oil are especially effective. Mix a few drops of the essential oil with water in a spray bottle, and spray your hair when you get out of the shower, while it's still wet. You can also spray your belongings with this to deter lice.

Use lice prevention shampoo and conditioners. These products usually contain the essential oils that deter lice and can be bought at drugstores.

Grooming

Keeping your hair clean is good hygiene; keeping it neat is good grooming! Come up with some easy, favorite ways to style your hair, and practice doing them on your own. Never leave the house without doing your hair. Neat-looking hair helps you look presentable.

5 EASY HAIRSTYLES FOR LONG HAIR

THE SIDE BRAID: Brush your hair so that it is tangle-free. Part your hair slightly to the side. Take a small portion of hair from the side of your part with the most hair, and braid. Secure at the bottom of the braid with a hair tie.

BRAIDED HALF-BACK: Take a small portion of hair on each side of your face and braid it, securing it with an elastic at the bottom. Bring both braids to the back of your head and secure them together as they meet in the middle. You can then take out the elastics at the bottom of each individual braid.

LOW PONY FLIP: Secure your hair with a hair band or an elastic in a low ponytail at the base of your skull. Pull the elastic down a bit further and create a hole right above it. Take the hair in your ponytail and thread it through the hole. Once the ponytail is flipped through, tug the opposite sides of it to tighten it up. This ponytail is secure and looks nice from the back.

HALF BUN: Divide your hair in half, top and bottom. Brush the top half of your hair, and wrap it in a bun at the top of your head. Secure with an elastic and bobby pins if needed.

FRENCH BRAIDS: Divide your hair into two sections, and secure one side with a hair tie for now. Starting at the top of your head, French braid the other side, gathering hair as you go, following the side of your head all the way down until the whole section is braided. Secure with a hair tie. Repeat on the other side. This is a great hairstyle for playing sports.

GETTING DRESSED

Getting dressed each day in neat clothing is a major part of good grooming. If any of your clothes are stained or ripped, see if you can fix them by applying a stain remover or mending the rip. If not, it could be time to use them as rags when cleaning. Choose clothes that are clean, in good condition, and wrinkle-free. How can you make sure this happens easily every day? Whether you dry your clothes in the dryer or hang them to dry on the line, pick them up as soon as they are finished drying. Hang or fold them immediately to prevent wrinkles in your clothes.

If you don't already have a place to store every category of clothing, create one. If you have a dresser, for example, the top drawer could be for socks and underwear, the second drawer could be for tops, the third drawer could be for bottoms (pants, shorts, leggings, skirts), and the bottom drawer could be for pajamas. You can hang dresses and coats in the closet. If there is no room for sweaters in your "tops" drawer, you can fold those and place them on a shelf separately. Avoid shoving your clothes into the drawers, but rather fold them neatly so that they will be wrinkle-free, not crumpled, when it comes time to get dressed.

Two Ways to Fold a T-Shirt

Traditional: Place your T-shirt face down on a flat surface, and smooth it out so that it does not have any wrinkles. Fold it in thirds, bringing the left side in and then the right side in. If the sleeves get in the way, you may fold them back out before folding the other side in. Now bring up the bottom of the shirt to meet the top. Turn it around, and you have a beautifully folded T-shirt.

Vertical fold: If you want to store your T-shirts vertically in your drawer so that you can see all of them at once, try this technique. As in the previous traditional fold, lay your T-shirt face down on a flat surface, and fold into thirds, tucking in the sleeves as needed. Now fold the T-shirt into thirds lengthwise from the top of the shirt to the bottom. Store it vertically among your other shirts in a drawer or basket.

How to Mend a Tear

You will need a needle and thread and the torn item of clothing. Make sure your thread will match your clothing so it can blend in and hide the mend. Place your thread through the eye of the needle and pull all the way until the bottom of the thread matches the other side. Tie a knot in the bottom of your thread.

Now take your threaded needle and, starting on the underside of the garment about ¼ inch [6 mm] away from the tear, pass your needle through the material. Go back through the material and sew up and down until you reach your tear. Once you reach the tear, you will start to pass the needle from opposite sides of the tear to ensure that it closes up. Start on one side of the tear, and cross over the tear to the other side. Pass the needle through the underside and repeat crossing over the tear, until you have sewn up the entire tear. Continue to sew ¼ inch [6 mm] above the tear, and finish on the underside of the garment. Snip the thread, leaving enough to tie into a double knot. Your tear is fixed!

Homemade Stain Remover

Because you are working with hydrogen peroxide,
have a parent help you make this stain remover.

Makes ¾ cup [180 ml]

3 tablespoons baking soda
¼ cup [60 ml] dish soap
½ cup [120 ml] hydrogen peroxide

Place the baking soda into a labeled spray bottle. Then add the dish soap and hydrogen peroxide to your bottle. You may use a funnel if needed. Use a dark-colored spray bottle because hydrogen peroxide degrades in light. Now close the cap tightly and shake. Spray the affected area, and scrub in the stain remover. Then wash the garment by hand or in the washing machine.

Daily Dressing Motivation

Why should we bother to get dressed every day? Why can't we stay in our pajamas all day long? After all, they're so comfortable! When you get dressed for the day, you are making yourself ready for whatever comes. You will feel presentable and not lazy. You are showing respect for yourself and those around you. Whether you wear a uniform to school or you choose your own clothes for the day, rejoice in getting dressed! When you get dressed, it means another day is here. What will be in store for you today?

Keep neatness in mind while you're getting dressed. When you take off your pajamas, place them in the dirty clothes hamper if they are dirty. If you plan to wear them again tonight, you can fold them and place them under your pillow.

When choosing your clothes for the day, only bring out what you plan to wear. If you are undecided, make sure you put away all of the clothes you brought out that you didn't end up choosing. Remember, we are not going to stuff our clothes in the drawers, but take a few seconds to fold and place them neatly in the drawer. Now that our rooms are kept tidy on a regular basis, we don't want to ever leave clothes, clean or dirty, in piles on the floor. Make sure all stray clothes are put away in their proper place.

When choosing what to wear, always consider the weather. If it's a cold day, you'll want to cover up and bundle up. If it's going to be warm, you will need fewer layers. If you're not sure, dress in layers, and if it warms up as the day goes on, you can take off your sweater.

WEAR YOUR SOCKS

Did you ever have one of those days when you were rushing to get your shoes on and decided to not wear socks? Apart from making your feet feel cozy, wearing socks with your sneakers or boots is actually an important part of everyday hygiene. Wearing socks prevents foot odor because they absorb the sweat that comes out of your feet. If you didn't wear socks, that sweat would go straight into your shoe. Because you wash your socks and not your shoes, your shoes would remain smelly from the body sweat. Wearing socks can even prevent fungal infections and athlete's foot. So whenever you wear closed-toed shoes, always wear your socks, too.

- CONNOISSEUR KIDS ASSIGNMENT -

PRACTICE GOOD HYGIENE

Become more aware of good hygiene and grooming through the lessons in this chapter. Give yourself enough time to get ready each morning so you don't need to rush. Brushing your teeth, cleaning your body, keeping your hands and nails clean, grooming your hair, and dressing neatly will help you go far. Being clean and looking neat are the keys to good hygiene and grooming.

I Have Nothing to Wear!

Have you ever looked into your closet and declared you had nothing to wear? Sometimes the problem is you have too many choices. Go through your clothes regularly, and pull out items that you no longer wear and that don't fit you. Remember the charity bag challenge from the chapter on tidying? You can donate your old clothes to a charity shop so that someone else can wear them. This will free up room in your closet and provide less choice. It will be easier to get dressed in the morning when you only choose between a few outfits.

My mother told me to get dressed.
I went to my closet and am stressed.
I have no idea what I will wear.
There's too much to choose from.
I'm in despair!
"I have nothing to wear, Mom!" I confessed.
She said, "Darling, you still must get dressed."

Choose your outfit the night before, and lay it out so in the morning you have already made your choice and don't even need to think about it. Check the weather report, and decide accordingly.

CHAPTER

6

HEALTH

Parents, the goals in this chapter are to: 1. Learn about leading a healthy lifestyle; 2. Practice a healthy lifestyle on a daily basis; and 3. Enjoy making healthy choices.

Our bodies are truly amazing, and that's why we need to take care of them as best we can. A Connoisseur Kid knows that a healthy lifestyle is the best way to live. What we eat, how we exercise, and even how we rest are vital parts of functioning every day.

YOUR HEALTH

Think back to a time when you were really sick. Maybe you had a fever and a terrible cough. You probably felt miserable and barely wanted to get out of bed. Feeling sick is the opposite of feeling healthy. The more you choose to take care of your body, the stronger your body will be. Your immune system, which protects your body against infection and contributes to your overall health, will grow stronger and you'll get sick less often if you start to develop healthy habits today.

5 AMAZING FACTS ABOUT THE IMMUNE SYSTEM

1. Your immune system is made up of organs, cells, and tissues.

2. Each part of your immune system has a specific function and purpose.

3. If you don't get enough sleep, your immune system is affected in a negative way.

4. Stress can cause damage to your immune system.

5. Laughter can help boost your immune system! Laughing releases dopamine in the brain, which can reduce stress. Dopamine is a chemical messenger that carries information between brain cells.

You know you want to live a healthy lifestyle to keep your immune system in good shape, but how can you do it? We are going to look at eating healthful foods, exercising regularly, getting enough sleep, and combatting stress with relaxation and plenty of laughter. Start these habits while you're young, and you will be on track for a healthy lifestyle for the rest of your life.

EATING WELL

French politician and well-known *gastronome* (a person who studies food) Jean Anthelme Brillat-Savarin, who was born in 1755, penned the famous quote, "Tell me what you eat, and I shall tell you what you are." In other words, you are what you eat! What do you think Monsieur Brillat-Savarin meant by this phrase?

He didn't mean that if we ate broccoli we would actually turn into broccoli. He meant to be fit and healthy, you must eat good food. If you run on junk food all day long, for example, and never have a real meal, you start to feel sick by the end of the day. Eating nothing but candy bars, doughnuts, and sodas all day long might seem like a dream come true, but in reality, you would grow tired of all of the sugary sweets and want some of your parents' home cooking to help you feel better. Monsieur Brillat-Savarin knew that if you eat poor-quality junk foods, you will probably feel tired, unhealthy, and listless. If you eat foods that are high in nutrients, you will have a lot of energy and abundant health. As you go throughout your day, remember that you are what you eat, so let's eat well!

5 FAVORITE MEALS

Write down your top 5 favorite meals and share them with your parents so they know what you love to eat. It can be anything from pancakes to tacos. Then ask them if you can follow along the next time they make your favorite meals so you can learn how to make them.

1. _____

2. _____

3. _____

4. _____

5. _____

- SPOTLIGHT ON -

JEAN ANTHELME BRILLAT-SAVARIN

Jean Anthelme Brillat-Savarin (1755–1826) was a French politician and gastronome whose famous book, Physiologie du goût (The Physiology of Taste), *published in 1825, is still revered and in print today. Brillat-Savarin's philosophy on food centered around joy and the pleasures of a good meal. Monsieur Brillat-Savarin had a healthy attitude toward food that can inspire us all to enjoy each meal.*

The Food Groups

Have you heard about food groups? The five important food groups are dairy, grains, fruits, meats (proteins), and vegetables. To eat a balanced diet, doctors recommend you eat from the five food groups each day. The best way to begin is to recognize which foods fall into which categories. Take a walk through your kitchen and have a look at your pantry and refrigerator. Note which category the items you see would go in. For example, milk, yogurt, cottage cheese, and string cheese would all be under the dairy category. Try to find five to ten items for each category in your kitchen. You might encounter some foods that don't fall into any of those categories. What about potato chips, cupcakes, and candy? These foods are OK to have in moderation—a small amount every once in a while—but they should never take up the bulk of our eating. We must be disciplined with ourselves and not overeat these snack and sweet foods.

Making Wise Food Choices

Remember Monsieur Brillat-Savarin's advice that suggested you are what you eat? We must strive to make wise food choices as Connoisseur Kids so that we are healthy, fit, and full of life. If you are used to craving junk food, you just need to change your mind and act on it. Instead of reaching for a bag of chips and a candy bar as a snack, you can reach for an apple or carrot sticks with hummus. Eating healthy food will help you with everything from boosting your immune system to focusing more at school, to playing better on the field.

Have you ever known someone who trained for a marathon? Maybe your mom or dad or aunt or uncle has run in a marathon. Ask them how they prepared. I bet in addition to running several times a week, they also tried to eat healthful foods as much as possible. They can tell you that what you eat truly does fuel your body for better or for worse.

One great tip for eating healthy is to eat your colors. Notice the abundance of color in fruits and vegetables: red strawberries, purple eggplant, green spinach, yellow bell peppers, deep red beets, orange carrots, blue blueberries. When you eat food that is naturally colorful, you are eating foods high in antioxidants (which protect your cells) and dense in nutrients.

Here is a helpful chart that shows what each color food can help with.*

COLOR	BENEFIT
Red	Helps heart and blood health and improves joints
Orange	Prevents cancer and promotes collagen growth
Yellow	Helps heart, vision, and digestion and boosts the immune system
Green	Detoxes, fights free radicals (which lead to cellular damage), and boosts the immune system
Blue and purple	Improves mineral absorption and contains powerful antioxidants
White	Activates natural killer cells and reduces cancer risk

Can you think which fruits and vegetables would fall under each color category? List some for each category so you know which ones you should try to add to your diet regularly.

Check out the following food chart to see how many you guessed correctly.

* Information from: DrJockers.com, "The Unique Benefits of Eating Colorful Foods," www.drjockers.com/benefits-eating-colorful-foods.

COLOR	FRUITS AND VEGETABLES
Red	Strawberries, pomegranate, red bell pepper, radishes, red cabbage, beets, raspberries, red apples, cranberries, rhubarb, red grapes, tomatoes, watermelon, cherries
Yellow	Yellow bell peppers, lemons, bananas, pineapple, corn, yellow tomatoes
Orange	Sweet potato, butternut squash, carrots, grapefruit, oranges, pumpkin, cantaloupe, papaya, mango
Green	Spinach, kale, lettuce, arugula, broccoli, green beans, peas, Swiss chard, collard greens, asparagus, zucchini, cucumber
Blue and purple	Blueberries, beets, eggplant, blackberries, purple grapes
White	Onions, garlic, turnips, cauliflower

When trying to decide what to eat,
Look for foods that are colorful, like a beet.
On broccoli, pears, and bell peppers, do nosh.
Same with strawberries, spinach,
And butternut squash.
Learn to enjoy your veggies and fruits,
And you will give your health
A much-needed boost.

CREATE YOUR OWN MENU

In this fun activity, you are going to create your own healthy menu. You will need a small poster board, markers, and a scratch piece of paper to work on. Take out your scratch paper and a pencil. Write down four categories: breakfast, lunch, snack, and dinner. Now you are going to brainstorm your ideal healthy menu. Try to include one food group in each meal. Pretend this is a menu at a restaurant. When you have come up with your menus, take out your poster board and markers and create a realistic-looking menu, the kind you'd see in a restaurant. You can hang this on the back of a kitchen cupboard or pantry door for healthy eating inspiration. Don't forget to name your restaurant!

Here are some sample meal ideas:

Breakfast: Scrambled eggs, whole wheat toast, turkey bacon, and fresh fruit with vanilla yogurt

Lunch: Turkey sandwich on whole wheat bread with lettuce, tomato, and cheese, served with sliced peaches and a glass of milk

Snack: Apple slices with peanut butter dipping sauce

Dinner: Roast chicken with peas and mashed potatoes with gravy and a side salad

For your menu, come up with as many meals as you can that include the important food groups. This might also give inspiration to the rest of the family to choose items off of your menu when they are planning meals.

Start the Day Off Right

The best way to start the day right, health-wise, is to eat a healthy breakfast. A healthy breakfast refuels your body after not eating all night and will give you the energy to enjoy your day. Have you ever wondered why we call the first meal of the day "breakfast"? If you break up the word, you see two words: "break" and "fast." A fast is when you don't do something for a long period of time, usually eating. When you fast, you are not eating food. You might sleep for 8 to 10 hours every night, and during that time you are also fasting because you aren't eating. When you wake up in the morning and have a meal, you are breaking the fast—in other words, breakfast!

Breakfast is one of the most important meals you'll eat all day, so make a healthy choice every morning. Avoid eating sugary cereals and sugary pastries. Of course, it's OK to have a doughnut for breakfast on special occasions, but on a daily basis, try eating foods that will fuel you, not make you feel hyper and drain your energy. Pancakes, waffles, and French toast are other sweet favorites and can be enjoyed in moderation once or twice a week.

Check out this healthy breakfast chart for ideas for your breakfasts, and write your own ideas below. Share this with your parents so you can all have new ideas for breakfast each morning:

HEALTHY BREAKFAST IDEAS

Hot oatmeal with chopped fruit and milk

Scrambled eggs with fruit and toast

Breakfast sandwich with sausage and egg

Smoothie bowl with granola

Fruit and yogurt parfait with granola

Avocado on toast with salt and pepper

Poached eggs on toast

Bran muffin with fruit

Breakfast burrito

Overnight oats with fruit and maple syrup

Slow Cooker Oatmeal

This is a delicious, healthy breakfast that cooks itself overnight! You'll wake up to breakfast already made—just scoop out of the slow cooker into a bowl and eat.

Serves 4

1 cup [80 g] old-fashioned or steel-cut oats (not instant oatmeal)

4 cups [960 ml] water

1 tablespoon chia seeds (optional)

Toppings of choice: sweetener (brown sugar or maple syrup), chopped fruit, almond milk or regular milk, chopped nuts, etc.

In your slow cooker the night before, combine the oatmeal, water, and chia seeds (if using). Place the lid on the slow cooker and cook on low for 8 to 10 hours. When you wake up in the morning, there will be oatmeal for everyone in your family. Make a double batch if you need to feed more people. Scoop the hot oatmeal into a bowl, and add your favorite toppings. You could be in charge of making this easy breakfast one or two days a week. It's very simple to do and so delicious!

Overnight Oats

*If you don't have a slow cooker, you can still make oatmeal over-
night with this recipe. Overnight oats is a small jar of oatmeal,
eaten cold with your favorite toppings. Eating cold oatmeal might
not sound very appetizing, but try this delicious treat and you
might be hooked! Here's how you make one jar of overnight oats.
Experiment tonight, and wake up tomorrow to see if you like it. You
will need a small Mason jar or a drinking glass.*

Serves 1

½ cup [40 g] old-fashioned or steel-cut oats
(not instant oatmeal)

½ cup [120 ml] milk or almond milk

¼ cup [60 g] plain or vanilla yogurt

2 or 3 tablespoons fruit, such as chopped strawberries, blueberries,
blackberries, or raspberries

1 teaspoon chia seeds (optional)

1 teaspoon maple syrup to sweeten

Dash of vanilla extract

Mix everything in a jar, cover, and refrigerate overnight. When
you wake up in the morning, you will have a healthy breakfast
waiting for you.

Easy Scrambled Eggs

You might need the assistance of an adult for this recipe, as you'll be using the stove.

Serves 1 or 2

2 eggs
2 tablespoons milk
Salt and pepper to taste
1 tablespoon butter

Crack your eggs into a bowl and add the milk, salt, and pepper. With a wire whisk, mix the eggs until they are broken up and totally blended. If you would like to make eggs for your whole family, add more eggs and more milk (2 eggs per adult and 1 egg per child is the general portion size). Place a medium-size skillet over medium-low heat. It's important not to have the heat too high. Melt the butter in the skillet. Once the butter is melted, pour your beaten egg mixture into the pan. An adult might have to help you with this part. Stay with your eggs because they cook quickly. Taking a spoon or large fork, stir the eggs as they cook, breaking them up, or "scrambling," them. You don't need to constantly stir them, but do so every 20 to 30 seconds. As soon as they look like they are turning solid and not runny, take them off the stove. You don't want to cook them for too long. Voilà—the perfect scrambled eggs.

Smoothie Bowls

To make a smoothie bowl, make your favorite smoothie and just use less liquid to make it thicker. Smoothies usually consist of your favorite fresh or frozen fruit, a milk (such as almond milk), and a banana. Pour it into a bowl and top with your favorite toppings, such as chopped fruit, chopped nuts, granola, and flaked coconut. Eat with a spoon and enjoy every refreshing bite! Wonderful combinations are strawberry banana, peach banana, blueberry banana, mixed berry banana, and pineapple mango banana. You could also add fresh spinach to any smoothie bowl to make it even healthier. For more smoothie recipes, see the "Fun with Fruits" section (page 180).

Avocado Toast

Do you love avocados? Avocados are loaded with potassium, healthy fats, and fiber. Eat them for breakfast and feel great all day long.

Serves 1

1 piece whole-grain bread
½ avocado
Salt and pepper to taste
Sprinkle of nutritional yeast (optional)

Toast your bread in the toaster. When it's finished, smash the avocado on the bread until it is smooth. Top with salt and pepper, and cover with a thin layer of nutritional yeast (this part is optional, but it provides a great flavor). Enjoy!

Best Bran Muffins

You'll need an adult to help with this recipe, because you'll be using the oven.

Makes 12 muffins

1½ cups [170 g] wheat bran
1 cup [240 ml] buttermilk
⅓ cup [80 ml] vegetable oil
1 egg
⅓ cup [90 g to 130 g] brown, white, or coconut sugar
½ teaspoon vanilla extract
1 cup [120 g] all-purpose flour
1 teaspoon baking soda
1 teaspoon baking powder
½ teaspoon salt
½ cup [60 to 90 g] chopped dates, raisins, or dried cranberries

Preheat your oven to 375°F [190°C]. Line a muffin tin with paper cups. In a large bowl, mix together the wheat bran and buttermilk. Set aside. In a separate bowl, beat the oil, egg, sugar, and vanilla, and add to the buttermilk mixture. Beat in the flour, baking soda, baking powder, and salt. Mix until incorporated. Fold in the chopped dates. Divide the mixture evenly among the paper liners. Bake for 15 to 20 minutes, or until a toothpick inserted into the center of a muffin comes out clean. Remove from the oven, and let them cool on a wire rack. Have an adult help you when using the oven. Always use oven mitts when putting something in or pulling something out of the oven. Once cool, transfer the muffins to freezer bags and freeze them. Take one muffin out to thaw at night to enjoy for breakfast the next day.

Enjoying Vegetables

Maybe you like fruit but have never cared much for vegetables. How can you add them to your diet and not be miserable? Enjoying vegetables is all about how you eat them. Serve them with yummy dips, sauces, and dressings, and you will not only learn to love them, but crave them, too!

Crudité Platter

A crudité (pronounced croo-dee-tay) platter is a plate of raw vegetables, usually served with a dip. You've probably seen many of these dishes (also known as veggie trays) at parties. The key to a good crudité platter is in the dip itself. A delicious dip can make raw veggies taste sensational! Not only is this platter great for parties or when you have company over, but it also makes a great everyday snack. When you are eating it as a snack, you only need to assemble a few of your favorite veggies, maybe two celery sticks and four carrot sticks, for example. A large crudité platter can include celery, broccoli, cauliflower, cherry tomatoes, bell or sweet peppers, carrots, sliced zucchini, and cucumber, but truly it can have any raw vegetable you like. Here are a few delicious dip recipes. These are easy to make. Just assemble the ingredients and mix!

Ranch Dip

Probably the most famous dip for veggies, ranch dip is a crowd-pleaser and adds a great flavor to your vegetables.

Makes 2 cups [480 g]

1 packet [1 ounce, or 28 g] dry ranch seasoning
2 cups [480 g] sour cream

In a bowl, mix the seasoning with the sour cream until combined. Enjoy!

Guacamole

Chips and guacamole are always delicious, but did you know that guacamole makes vegetables taste great, too? Here is a simple guacamole recipe. Feel free to add extras to it like chopped tomato to make it chunkier.

Makes about 2 cups [480 g]

2 ripe avocados
1 tablespoon lemon or lime juice
1 teaspoon salt
Pepper to taste
2 tablespoons finely chopped cilantro (optional)
½ tomato, finely chopped (optional)

Slice the avocados in half, avoiding the seed in the middle. (You will need the assistance of an adult for this.) Scoop out the avocado with a large spoon. Discard the seed. Place the avocados in a bowl with the lemon juice, salt, pepper, and cilantro (if using). Using a potato masher or the back of a fork, smash the avocados together with the rest of the ingredients. Add the chopped tomato at the end for a chunky texture, if desired.

French Onion Dip

This delicious, savory dip will tickle your taste buds and, like the ranch dip, is very easy to make.

Makes 2 cups [480 g]

2 cups [480 g] sour cream
1 packet [1 ounce, or 28 g] French onion soup mix

In a bowl, stir together the soup mix and sour cream until fully combined. Enjoy.

Spinach and Artichoke Dip

This warm dip requires more preparation, but it is so delicious, especially on a chilly day.

Makes about 4 cups [940 g]

1 can [14 ounces, or 784 g] artichoke hearts, drained
1 package [10 ounces, or 280 g] frozen chopped spinach, thawed and fully drained
¾ cup [75 g] grated Parmesan cheese
¾ cup [180 g] mayonnaise
½ cup [75 g] shredded mozzarella cheese
½ teaspoon garlic salt

Preheat the oven to 350°F [180°C]. Grease a small baking dish or pie pan. In a large bowl, mix all of the ingredients together until well blended. Scoop the mixture into the prepared baking dish. Bake for 15 to 20 minutes, until warmed through. Remove from the oven and let cool before using. Have an adult help you when using the oven. Always use oven mitts when putting something in or pulling something out of the oven.

Tzatziki Dip

The lemon juice adds a kick to this famous Greek dip, which makes a delicious contribution to any crudité platter.

Makes about 1½ cups [360 g]

1 cup [240 g] Greek yogurt
½ cucumber, finely chopped
2 tablespoons lemon juice
2 tablespoons chopped fresh dill
1 tablespoon white vinegar
Salt and pepper to taste

Place all the ingredients in a bowl, and stir until well combined. Have an adult help you with chopping the cucumber. Cover and let the dip chill in the refrigerator for 1 hour before eating. Enjoy!

Honey Mustard Dip

Honey mustard dip is another crowd-pleaser. Its unique taste will sweeten up any raw veggies you like to eat.

Makes about 1 cup [240 g]

½ cup [170 g] honey
⅓ cup [60 g] Dijon mustard
2 tablespoons apple cider vinegar

Place all the ingredients in a small saucepan on the stove over medium to low heat. Have an adult help you with the stove. Stir until slightly thickened. Serve and enjoy.

Fun with Fruits

Fruit is delicious when enjoyed all by itself, but sometimes it's fun to mix it up and try new recipes. Many of these fruity treats can be eaten for dessert, making a tasty end to a nice meal. Here are some great fruity recipes that will encourage you to eat your colors.

Yummy Yogurt Fruit Dip

Take inspiration from your new crudité dips, and try this one out next time you enjoy fruit. It's yummy and sweet.

Makes 1¼ cups [360 g]

1 cup [240 g] plain yogurt
¼ cup [85 g] honey
½ teaspoon vanilla extract
Dash of ground cinnamon

Mix all the ingredients together in a bowl. Enjoy dipping your favorite fruit in this delightful mix. Or drizzle on top of a bowl of your favorite chopped fruit.

Rainbow Fruit Kabobs

This is a fun way to eat a fruity snack. Use any combination of your favorite fruit, chopped into bite-size pieces. Mandarin orange, kiwi, mango, grapes, pineapple, bananas, and strawberries are good choices. Thread your favorite fruit onto a kabob stick, making a colorful rainbow. Serve these kabobs with the yummy fruit dip.

Strawberry Banana Smoothie

This classic smoothie is a great addition to any healthy eating program.

Serves 2

2 cups [300 g] strawberries (use frozen if they are out of season)
1 medium ripe banana
1 cup [240 ml] milk (you can also use almond milk)
½ cup [75 g] ice
1 tablespoon honey

Add all the ingredients to a blender and blend until smooth.

Serve in a tall glass with a straw, and enjoy drinking your fruits.

Green Peach Smoothie

This smoothie combines both fruits and a vegetable. You would never know it contains spinach if it weren't green!

Serves 2

1½ cups [260 g] chopped peaches, fresh or frozen
1 cup [240 ml] almond milk (or other milk)
1 cup [30 g] fresh spinach
1 medium banana
½ cup [120 g] vanilla or plain yogurt

Add all the ingredients to a blender and blend until smooth.

Enjoy this refreshing drink with a straw.

Mini Fruit Pizzas

Make these mini pizzas when you're craving a sweet snack.

Serves 3 or 4

3 or 4 flour or whole wheat tortillas
½ cup [120 g] plain yogurt
1 tablespoon honey
1 tablespoon orange juice
Dash of vanilla extract
Chopped fruit of your choice

Using a round cookie cutter, cut circles out of your tortillas. Set aside. In a bowl, mix together the yogurt, honey, orange juice, and vanilla. Spread the sauce on the tortilla circles, and top with your favorite fresh fruit. Delish!

Frozen Chocolate Banana Bites

These frozen treats are a delicious dessert and very fun to make.

Makes 12 bites

3 ripe bananas
1 cup [165 g] chocolate chips
Favorite toppings (sprinkles, shredded coconut, chopped peanuts)

Cut each banana in half and then in half again. You will have 12 pieces. Place toothpicks into each piece of banana, place on a baking sheet, and freeze until they are firm, about 1½ hours. Place the chocolate chips in a microwave-safe bowl and microwave on high for 10 seconds. Stir. Repeat in 10-second bursts until the chocolate is fully melted. Spread your toppings on a shallow plate. Hold the frozen bananas by their toothpicks and dip in the chocolate sauce, then immediately roll them in the topping. Refrigerate until ready to eat or enjoy right away.

No-Bake Coconut Chocolate Granola Bites

These granola bites are full of healthy nuts and fats, to fuel your brain all day long. Plus, you never even have to turn on the oven to make them!

Makes 24 bites

1 cup [80 g] old-fashioned oats (not instant oatmeal)
½ cup [60 g] ground flaxseed
½ cup [120 g] peanut butter
½ cup [85 g] mini chocolate chips
⅓ cup [115 g] honey
1 teaspoon vanilla extract
¼ cup [20 g] toasted, shredded coconut

Mix all of the ingredients together in a large bowl until well combined. Drop rounded tablespoon-size portions onto a cookie sheet lined with parchment paper. You should get about 24 bites. Refrigerate for 1 to 2 hours. To store, refrigerate in an airtight container for up to 1 week, or freeze for up to 3 months.

Yummy and Healthful Snacks

Snack time, usually between lunch and dinner, is normally a time when we are looking for something to satisfy our hunger in a tasty way. Snack time is also a time when we can make a poor choice and eat junky foods, instead of energy-boosting, healthful ones. Keep the list of healthy snack ideas that follows handy so that you will never be at a loss for what to have at snack time. Feel free to add your own ideas to this list as well.

However, it's important not to eat too many snacks throughout the day. Have you ever had one of those days where you snacked all day long and then weren't hungry for dinner? We want to make sure that we snack in moderation. That means that we control when we snack and that we don't do it too much. It is helpful to have set snack times during the day. For example, you probably have a snack time at school in the morning. When you get home from school is most likely another snack time. We don't want to snack all the way until dinner, however, because then we won't be hungry for dinner. Usually breakfast, lunch, and dinner contain the big food groups we discussed, so it's important to get those nutrients in. Some people like a small snack before bed, especially if they've eaten an early dinner.

Enjoy healthy snacks and avoid getting into bad snacking habits by setting designated snack times for yourself. Always choose the healthiest snack possible. There will always be special days when you enjoy a cupcake or ice pop instead of your usual snack. Enjoy those moments! On a regular basis, though, let's aim to snack well.

HEALTHFUL SNACK IDEAS

Fruit smoothie (page 181)

Sliced apples with almond butter

Air-popped popcorn with Parmesan cheese and salt

Tortilla chips with salsa or guacamole (page 177)

Avocado toast with salt and pepper (page 174)

Strawberry peanut butter crêpes (take a ready-made crêpe and spread with peanut butter and chopped strawberries)

Cottage cheese and fruit

A whole piece of fruit of your choice

Yogurt

A handful of almonds or another nut

Oatmeal cookie and milk

Raw veggies such as carrots and celery with your favorite crudité dip (pages 176–179)

Cheese with whole-grain crackers

Salami and cheese

Bran muffin (page 175)

No-bake granola bites (page 183)

DRINKING WATER

T hink of all the beverages there are in the world: coffee, tea, juice, soda, shakes, and the list could go on! While these special drinks are fun to have, do you know that you could get by your whole life without having any of them? But there is one drink you cannot live without, and that is water. Humans need to drink water to survive. Most of us don't drink enough water. We might go for a few sips every few hours when we feel thirsty, but truly we should be drinking many glasses of water a day. How many glasses exactly? Seven-to-eight-year-olds need 7 cups [1.7 L] of water a day and nine-to-twelve-year-olds need 8 to 10 cups [2 to 2.4 L] a day. That's almost drinking an entire glass of water every single hour!

Our days can be so busy that hours can go by and we realize we haven't had a drink of water. Here is a helpful idea to get you to drink what you need to in a day. You can fill a large water bottle with the exact amount of water you need. Aim to have it empty by the time you go to bed (see the chart on page 134). If you get halfway through the day and you realize you haven't had much of your water yet, you can drink extra. Staying hydrated with plenty of water has many health benefits. Water keeps your skin healthy and your joints in good condition and cleanses your body from the inside.

SWEETS AND SELF-CONTROL

Is dessert your favorite part of the meal? People who like desserts say they have a "sweet tooth." If someone says they have a sweet tooth, it means that the person loves sweet treats. Having a small dessert every day is OK. The important idea is to have self-control when you eat your sweets. Let's say it's a holiday, and you received a big basket of candy as a present. Your temptation might be to eat as much of the candy as possible. In the moment, it might seem like a good idea, and it might taste delicious, but a half hour later, you will feel terrible.

If you've ever overdone it with eating too many sugary foods, you've probably experienced the miserable feeling you get afterward.

What happens to your body when you eat too much sugar? There are many negative consequences for this. Here are a few.*

Eating too much sugar can cause tooth decay. Sugar interacts with the bacteria in your mouth and produces acid, which can cause your teeth to decay.

Eating too much sugar can cause problems with your skin via acne, rosacea, and other irritations.

Eating too much sugar has a direct link to weight gain. Sugary foods are usually high in calories. Eating a high-calorie diet can cause you to gain weight. What is a calorie? It's a unit of energy used to measure the amount of energy stored in food.

Eating too much sugar can lead to various diseases, such as heart and liver disease.

We now know that consuming too much sugar is harmful to the body, so we will always use self-control when enjoying sweets. Have one candy or one helping of dessert instead of two or three. Even if you really want more, exhibit self-control, and only have one helping. Take your time and enjoy that one treat you have. Eat it slowly, and give it your full attention. You will feel satisfied from your treat and not feel sick from overindulging.

Rich, moist chocolate cake and sticky sweet, glazed dough-nuts are always welcome desserts to eat, but did you know that yummy desserts can also be healthy, too? Try these recipes out when your sweet tooth kicks in, and enjoy them knowing you are eating a healthy dessert.

* Information from: Insider, "10 Scary Things That Happen to Your Body When You Eat Too Much Sugar," www.thisisinsider.com/ what-happens-when-you-eat-too-much-sugar-2017-9.

Blueberry Frozen Yogurt Pops

These healthy pops taste creamy and satisfying.

Makes 4 frozen pops

1 cup [240 g] plain yogurt

1 ripe banana

1 cup [160 g] frozen blueberries (or mixed berries)

2 tablespoons honey

Mix all the ingredients in a blender. Pour into ice pop molds. Freeze for 4 hours, or until solid.

Banana Ice Cream

Did you know you can make a delicious treat from frozen bananas that has the texture of soft-serve ice cream?

Serves 1 or 2

2 ripe bananas

Chop your bananas into smaller pieces, place them on a tray, and freeze for at least 2 hours. Place your frozen bananas in a blender or food processor. Blend until they are the consistency of ice cream. Scoop into a bowl and enjoy! You can experiment with this recipe by adding your favorite ingredients. Try adding ¼ cup [40 g] chocolate chips or a few crushed graham crackers for added texture.

No-Bake Chocolate Oat Bars

These oat bars are full of good-for-you ingredients and are made without the oven!

4 cups [720 g] pitted dates
½ cup [60 g] cocoa powder
1 cup [80 g] old-fashioned oats (not instant oatmeal)
1 cup [150 g] raw almonds, chopped into small pieces
½ cup [40 g] coconut flakes
½ cup [60 g] oat bran
1 teaspoon vanilla extract

Soak the dates in warm water for 12 minutes to soften them. Place the dates and cocoa powder in a food processor or blender and blend until combined. Place the date mixture into a large bowl and add the rest of the ingredients. If the mixture is too wet, you can add more chopped nuts. Feel free to use other kinds of nuts, such as cashews, walnuts, or pecans. Stir until fully combined. Line a baking sheet with wax paper. Place your mixture on the paper, and press down flat until it reaches the edges. Chill for at least 1 hour. When they are ready, cut into bar shapes. You can store these in a sealed container for up to 1 week. Enjoy!

Chocolate-Dipped Strawberries

These strawberries look very festive and would be a great treat for Valentine's Day!

Makes 12 strawberries

12 large strawberries

2 ounces [55 g] chocolate, chopped

¼ cup [20 to 40 g] crushed graham crackers, nuts, or sprinkles (optional)

Wash and dry your strawberries. Place the chocolate in a microwave-safe bowl. Microwave for 30 seconds at a time, stirring each time the microwave beeps. Microwave until your chocolate melts (usually around 90 seconds total). Spread your topping on a shallow plate (if using). Place a toothpick through the crown of the strawberry. Dip it in the melted chocolate. If desired, roll the chocolate-covered strawberry in the topping while the chocolate is still warm. Lay the strawberry down on clean wax paper. Repeat with the rest of the berries. The chocolate should harden after 20 minutes. These should be eaten the day they are made, so share them with your friends and family!

Baked Apples

This delicious dessert is perfect for fall, when the apples are crisp and the weather turns cooler. You'll need an adult to help you with the oven and coring the apples.

Serves 4

4 large baking apples
½ cup [40 g] old-fashioned oats (not instant oatmeal)
¼ cup [35 g] raisins (optional)
¼ cup [60 g] brown sugar
1 teaspoon ground cinnamon
2 tablespoons butter
1 cup [240 ml] boiling water

Preheat the oven to 350°F [180°C]. Wash and dry your apples. Have an adult help you core the apple at the top, leaving a hole for the stuffing. You do not want to go all the way to the bottom of the apple. Mix the oats, raisins, brown sugar, and cinnamon together in a bowl. Stuff the apples with the filling. Dot each apple with a pat of butter. Place in a baking dish and pour the boiling water in the bottom of the dish. Bake your apples for 45 to 50 minutes, until a toothpick inserted in the apple meets no resistance and the apple is soft all the way through. When they are finished, drizzle some of the juices from the pan on top of the apples. Enjoy alone or with a scoop of vanilla ice cream.

NEVER EAT ON THE GO

Never eat on the go. Always make sure you are seated properly at a table when eating your food. If you eat on the go, while walking, or in the car, you are more likely to eat more, beyond when you are naturally full. This is because you are not paying attention to what you are eating. You are doing multiple things at once: walking, eating, and maybe even talking! You might eat too fast and overindulge in your food. A great rule of thumb is to always sit down for each and every meal, even your snacks.

EXERCISE IS FUN!

When discussing health, you'll often notice that diet and exercise are mentioned together. Diet is what you eat, and exercise is working out your body through sports or other activities. It's important to exercise every single day, rain or shine.

Even if you play on a sports team, you will need to actively plan exercise in your life. There's always the down season and off days. Exercise should never be a chore. Getting out and moving your body should be fun. You can look forward to it! See the following page for some fun exercises for sunny days and rainy days.

OUTDOOR EXERCISE FOR SUNNY DAYS	INDOOR EXERCISE FOR RAINY DAYS
Swimming	Jump rope
Biking	Rebounding (mini trampoline)
Hiking	Jumping jacks
Walking	Push-ups
Tennis	Walking up and down the stairs
Running	Doing an exercise DVD
Golf	Stretching
Soccer, basketball, baseball, softball	Dancing to music
Tag	Lifting weights

Stretch!

Does your body ever feel stiff when you first wake up? A wonderful habit to get into is to stretch for a few minutes every morning before starting your day. You can even do this while you are still in your pajamas!

The benefits of stretching are many. You increase the circulation of your blood, become more flexible, reduce muscle tension, and boost your energy levels (from your increased circulation). Start your day with a few easy stretches and experience the benefits for yourself. Here are three easy stretches you can do.

Standing touch your toes. Stand up straight and, keeping your knees slightly bent, bend over at the waist as far as you can. See if you can touch your toes. Hang there for as long as you like, breathing deeply as you stretch.

Sitting touch your toes. Sit down on the floor with your legs stretched out straight in front of you. Bend your knees slightly. Raise your arms over your head and, breathing deeply, bend and bring your arms and head forward until your arms are touching your toes. If you cannot reach your toes, just go as far as you can. Breathe deeply and release.

Butterfly stretch. Sit on the floor with your legs stretched out straight in front of you. Now put the soles of your feet together. Lean forward, keeping your back as straight as possible, and rest your elbows on the sides of your legs. Breathe deeply.

- CONNOISSEUR KIDS ACTIVITY -
SPELL YOUR NAME EXERCISE

For a fun challenge that will get you moving, try this spell your name activity. Check out the key below. For each letter of your name, do the activity listed. If you have a long name, you'll be getting in quite the workout! Do this with friends and family for an added element of fun. This is great for rainy days!

A. 20 jumping jacks
B. 12 squats
C. 15 foward arm circles
D. 15 backward arm circles
E. 2-minute wall sit
F. 16 crunches
G. 15 squats
H. 10 push-ups
I. 24 jumping jacks
J. 12 high knees

K. Run in place for 2 minutes
L. 30-second plank
M. 14 lunges
N. Jump rope for 2 minutes
O. 15 high knees
P. 15 forward arm circles
Q. 18 leg lifts
R. Bicycle your legs for 2 minutes
S. Dance for 3 minutes
T. 20 crunches
U. 14 push-ups
V. 20 lunges
W. Run in place for 2 minutes
X. 2-minute wall sit
Y. 45-second plank
Z. 15 arm circles each direction

When you are exercising, make sure you are drinking plenty of water and resting when you need to. If you aren't sure how to do the exercises in the Spell Your Name activity, they are described here:

How to do arm circles:

Stand up straight and extend your arms out to the side. Slowly make circles 12 inches [30 cm] in diameter going forward. Breathe and make sure your knees are relaxed. Repeat going backward, if desired.

How to bicycle your legs:

Lie flat on your back and lift your legs into the air. Pump your legs in circular motions as if you were riding a bicycle.

How to do crunches:

Lie on your back with your bent knees hip-distance apart. Your feet should be flat on the floor. Put your arms behind your head, and lock your thumbs together. Tilt your chin toward your chest. Curl up slowly, leading by your abdominal (stomach) muscles. You don't need to go all the way up; only lift your head, neck, and shoulder blades off the ground. Lower down. Repeat.

How to do high knees:

Stand straight with your feet hip-distance apart. Extend your arms out, palms facing down, at your belly-button height. Quickly bring your right knee up to meet your right hand. As soon as your right leg goes back down, bring your left knee up to meet your left hand. Repeat.

How to do leg lifts:

Lie down on your left side, one leg on top of the other, with your head resting on your outstretched arm. Slowly lift your right leg as high as possible and then lower it back down. Repeat. When you are ready, switch to the right side and do the same with your left leg.

How to do lunges:

Stand straight with your shoulders back and look forward. Extend your right leg in front of you, lowering your hips until both knees are bent at a 90-degree angle. Your front knee should be directly above your ankle. Push back up to standing and repeat on the left leg.

How to do push-ups:

Lie down facing the ground with your hands and the tops of your feet the only body parts touching the floor. Keep your body from your legs to your neck and head in a straight line. Your hands should be shoulder-width apart. Gently lower down, bending your elbows as far as you can go and then press up again. If you need to, place your knees on the ground for extra support.

How to do a plank:
Get into a push-up position (see previous exercise), but instead of having your hands on the floor, you will have your forearms on the floor, forming a 90-degree angle. Keep your neck straight. Hold this position for as long as you can, pulling in your belly and keeping your back straight.

How to do squats:
Stand with your feet hip-distance apart and put your hands on your hips. Slowly sink down, bending your knees and hips. Keep your back straight and never let your knees go over your toes. Sink as low as possible, and then slowly come up. Repeat.

How to do a wall sit:
Place your back flat against a wall. Spread your feet shoulder-width apart, and scoot them 12 to 24 inches [30 to 60 cm] out from the wall. Slide your back down the wall, bending your legs until they form a 90-degree angle. It will look like you're sitting in an invisible chair! Hold this position. Release.

How to do jumping jacks:
Stand up straight with your feet together and your hands by your sides. In one smooth motion, jump your feet out wide, and bring your hands up to clap them over your head. In another smooth motion, jump your feet back together, and bring your hands back down to your sides. Repeat.

ROUTINES

Establishing everyday routines is a great way to seal in your healthy habits. Routines are a sequence of actions that are regularly followed. Some people may think routines are boring, but routines can add an anchor to your day. You will always know what to expect, and you can refine all of the wonderful skills you are learning through regular practice by incorporating them into your routines.

Morning Routine

The most important routine to have is a morning routine. Do you have a morning routine? If you already do, write your morning routine down on a sheet of paper. You can see where you can add steps or take away unnecessary steps. Your goal each morning is to start the day off right with healthy habits, incorporating all of the Connoisseur Kid tips you've been practicing.

Here is a sample morning routine:

Wake up at 7 a.m.
Use the restroom.
Brush your teeth.
Stretch for 2 minutes.
Drink a tall glass of water.
Make your bed.
Get dressed, putting your dirty clothes away properly.
Wash your face and brush your hair.
Apply sunscreen, if needed.
Make sure your nails are clean.
Go to the kitchen for breakfast.
Eat a healthy breakfast.
Gather your belongings for school.

This is a very basic morning routine list. You can change it in any way to fit your lifestyle best. You want to hit all of the major points: hygiene and grooming (brushing teeth, brushing hair, washing face, applying sunscreen, and dressing in neat clothing), tidiness (making the bed and putting your pajamas away), and health (stretching in the morning, drinking plenty of water, and eating a healthy breakfast). Your goal is to get ready for the day and to enjoy doing so. It may seem easier to just roll out of bed and go downstairs for breakfast while you hang out in your pajamas (and you can totally do that on the weekends), but when you have to get ready for school or other important events, start your day off right by implementing a weekday morning routine.

Evening Routine

After a long day, look forward to your trusty evening routine to get you ready for bed. After dinner cleanup and evening activities (such as practicing an instrument, doing homework, playing games, etc.) are over, head to your bedroom to get ready for bed. Many people take a bath or shower at night. If you take one in the morning, you can add that to your morning routine. Here is a sample evening routine:

Put away your clothes for the day in the dirty clothes hamper.
Take a bath or shower.
Apply lotion to your skin.
Brush your teeth.
Drink your final glass of water for the day.
Check your nails and clean or cut them, if necessary.
Brush your hair and put it in braids, if necessary.
Lay out your clothes for tomorrow.
Look around your room and tidy up any areas that are in need.
Get into bed with a good book.
Read.
Fall asleep.

Tailor your nighttime routine to your specific needs. The key is consistency. That means doing your routine regularly. If you get established with a good nighttime routine, by taking care of hygiene and grooming, tidiness, and preparing for the next day, you will set yourself up for a great tomorrow.

RESTING

When your day is full of action, you also need lots of rest. Connoisseur Kids between the ages of six and thirteen need 9 to 11 hours of sleep each night.* Establish a good bedtime routine for yourself, and aim to go to bed at the same time each night to make sure you get enough sleep.

When should your bedtime be? Let's move forward to the morning to answer that question. What time do you need to wake up each morning to get ready for school? To establish your wake-up time, keep in mind how long it takes you to get dressed, brush your teeth, groom yourself, eat breakfast, and travel to school. Then count back 11 hours—that would be the time you should go to bed. For example, if you need to wake up at 7:00 a.m. each day, you would need to go to bed at 8:00 p.m. the evening before.

If you are used to staying up later than your ideal bedtime, slowly, night by night, go to bed a little earlier than before.

* Information from: National Sleep Foundation, "How Much Sleep Do We Really Need?," www.sleepfoundation.org/how-sleep-works/how-much-sleep-do-we-really-need.

In order to nod off to sleep peacefully, avoid all screens: television, tablets, phones, and any other technology you like to use, at least 2 hours before bed. Playing video games or watching television shows can stimulate your brain and make you feel awake, not sleepy. To keep yourself occupied before bedtime, do gentle crafts or coloring. After you relax with these activities, the absolute best thing to do is read in bed until it's time to go to sleep. Have a good bedside lamp to illuminate your book properly and read, read, read.

Reading regularly not only improves your memory and mental abilities, but it also fights against sleeplessness, or insomnia. Reading before bed helps your body relax and, after a while, can make you very sleepy.* So gather some exciting books and keep them in your room. You are going to establish a new reading routine before falling asleep each night.

When the moon rises up and it's time to sleep,
Head to your bed, but don't count sheep.
Instead pick up a book and read into the night.
You will feel relaxed when you turn out the light.
You'll fall into a deep and peaceful rest
And wake up refreshed, ready to do your best.

* Information from: *Business Insider*, "The Surprising Benefits of Reading Before Bed," www.businessinsider.com/the-surprising-benefits-of-reading-before-bed-2015-8.

Nighttime sleep is very important, but what about resting during the day? If you have a little brother or sister, you know that they take a nap each day. Small children need even more sleep, so they will often nap for a few hours each afternoon. You might be too old to take a nap, but that doesn't mean you can't rest. Listen to your body. If you've had a long day at school and playing sports, a rest might be in order. How can you rest if you don't nap? You can lie down and read, chat with a family member, or listen to music. You can do a relaxing craft or do a hobby that comforts you, like playing the piano or painting. Give yourself some downtime that allows your brain and your body to rest.

ENTERTAINMENT AND RELAXATION

Television, movies, video games, and apps: these forms of entertainment are in high demand! You might enjoy watching your favorite show or playing on a tablet every now and then, but we should not spend too much time entertaining ourselves this way. A Connoisseur Kid knows that getting out and experiencing life, not virtual reality behind a screen, is a more fulfilling way to live.

Reading for Fun

Regarding entertainment, we should spend more time reading each day than we do watching a screen. Reading actively engages your mind and imagination. The benefits of reading are vast! Take a look at the following list showing the benefits of reading.

BENEFITS OF READING

Increases intelligence: Reading exposes you to more words than television and improves your vocabulary and spelling.

Helps you relax: Reading can reduce your stress by up to 68 percent, according to a 2009 study by Sussex University.

Makes you a better writer: Not only will your vocabulary and spelling improve, but reading will also inspire your own writing.

Improves your analytical skills: If you're reading a mystery and trying to solve it before the book is finished, for example, you are analyzing what you're reading. Good critical and analytical skills are great life skills to have.

Boosts concentration: With all of the screen time we face each day, our eyes and attention can flit from one thing to another quickly. Sitting down and reading a good book improves our concentration and focus.

Improves school performance: The more you read, the better you do in school. We know reading improves our vocabulary, spelling, comprehension, analytical skills, and critical thinking skills.

- CONNOISSEUR KIDS ASSIGNMENT -

MAKE TIME FOR READING

Establish a reading time every day. It could be 40 minutes before you go to sleep, or any other time of day. Find a cozy, well-lit spot to read your book where you won't be disturbed. During the summertime you could read out in the hammock or even in a tree! During the winter, cozy up in the armchair by the fireplace, and get lost in a book. Establish your reading spots and reading times. Visit your local library regularly so you always have your next book ready. Get wild about reading, and see the benefits flourish in your life.

Feeling Bored?

If you ever feel bored and at a loss for what to do, here is a list of 50 activities you can do instead of watching screens. Fill in your own ideas at the bottom of the list. Customize the list for your life.

50 ACTIVITIES TO DO INSTEAD OF WATCHING SCREENS

Bake a cake or some cookies.

Learn how to scramble eggs (page 173).

Make homemade play dough (page 211).

Make slime (pages 212–213).

Climb a tree.

Ride a bike, scooter, or skateboard, or roller-skate.

Go on a hike.

Create a treasure hunt and map for your friends to go on.

Read a book.

Write a book.

Write a poem.

Plant some seeds.

Pick flowers.

Weed the garden.

Play "school."

Play "shop."

Learn woodwork.

Put on a play.

Put on a dance show.

Put on a circus.

Do a puppet show.

Paint with watercolors.

Draw on the sidewalk with chalk.

Make the world's longest hopscotch board.

Jump rope.

Play "restaurant."

Build a pillow fort.

Put a tent in the backyard and go camping.

Go swimming.

Lean to make your favorite meal.

Memorize the 50 states and know where they are on the map.

Make bath bombs (page 214).

Go to the library.

Learn how to play an instrument.

Make pizza from scratch.

Learn how to sew.

Play board games.

Write letters to family members.

Learn how to play chess.

Learn a new sport like golf or tennis.

Plant a window box.

Take the dog on a walk.

Clean the fish tank.

Organize your bedroom.

Flip through a colorful cookbook.

Write down your own jokes.

Do a word search or crossword puzzle.

Create your own maze on paper for someone else to solve.

Make homemade frozen yogurt pops (page 189).

Run through the sprinklers.

Homemade Play Dough

Making your own play dough is fun and easy to do.
If stored properly in an airtight container or zip-top bag,
this play dough lasts a long time, too!

Makes 4 cups

2 cups [480 ml] water
1 cup [280 g] salt
2 tablespoons vegetable oil
2 tablespoons cream of tartar
2 cups [240 g] all-purpose flour
Food coloring

Combine the water, salt, oil, and cream of tartar in a saucepan
and heat until warm. You will need an adult to help you with
this. Remove from the heat and add the flour. Mix with a spoon.
Transfer to a cutting board and knead the dough. Divide into four
balls. Add a different color to each ball with food coloring. Knead
the dough until the color is incorporated well. The cream of tartar
in this recipe makes the play dough last a long time. Store in a
labeled airtight container to keep it moist. Enjoy!

Basic Slime Recipe

This translucent slime is so easy to make and fun to play with.

½ cup [120 ml] clear glue
½ teaspoon baking soda
1 drop food coloring
Glitter, confetti, or scented oil (optional)
2 to 3 tablespoons contact lens solution
Cooking spray

In a bowl, combine the clear glue, baking soda, and food coloring. Mix. If you would like to add additional ingredients like glitter, confetti, or scent, do so now. Finally, add the contact lens solution while mixing. Stir until the slime forms a lump and no longer sticks to the sides of the bowl. Spray lightly with cooking spray to avoid having sticky slime. Store in a labeled airtight container.

Fluffy Slime

The secret ingredient to this slime is shaving cream,
which gives it a fluffy consistency.

⅓ cup [80 ml] hot water
1 teaspoon borax
1 cup [240 ml] white glue
½ cup [120 ml] cool water
3 cups [210 g] shaving cream
2 tablespoons contact lens solution
3 to 4 drops food coloring (optional)
Cooking spray

In a small bowl, combine the hot water and borax. Stir until the
borax is dissolved and the water is clear. Set aside. In a large
bowl, combine the glue and cool water. Mix. Then add the shaving
cream (or more, if needed) and mix. Add the contact lens solution
and stir to combine. If you would like colored slime, add the food
coloring. Mix in 2 to 3 tablespoons [30 to 45 ml] of the borax
solution, 1 tablespoon [15 ml] at a time. Continue to stir until
your slime forms into a large clump and pulls away from the sides
of the bowl. Spray lightly with cooking spray so the slime is not
sticky. Store in a labeled airtight container. (You won't use all of
the borax solution; save for another batch in a labeled airtight
container.)

Note: Make sure to keep your Fluffy Slime away from your pets.
Borax isn't good for them (or you!) to eat.

DIY Bath Bombs

Bath bombs add sparkle and fizz to your bath time. These are so fun to use! This recipe was adapted from Swanson Health Products.

½ cup [65 g] baking soda

¼ cup [35 g] cornstarch

¼ cup [60 g] Epsom salts

¼ cup [30 g] citric acid

3 to 4 teaspoons [15 to 20 g] coconut oil, melted

1 to 2 teaspoons water

1 teaspoon favorite essential oil (lavender, peppermint, or lemon works great)

Food coloring (optional)

In a bowl, combine the baking soda, cornstarch, Epsom salts, and citric acid. In another bowl, combine the coconut oil, water, essential oil, and food coloring (if using). Slowly add the wet ingredients to the dry, stirring with a whisk until fully mixed together. (If you want to use different colors, to create a swirl effect, divide the mixtures up into different batches.) When the mixture looks like it's wet enough to stick together in clumps, press it firmly into bath bomb molds until the molds are filled. (Or you could use silicone ice cube trays or other silicone molds.) Remove any excess from the sides. Let the mixture sit in the molds for 5 to 10 minutes, then carefully remove them and let them dry for 24 hours before using.

LAUGHTER

We are working on establishing healthy lifestyle routines through good eating, exercise, sound sleep, and non-screen hobbies, but did you know that laughter is an essential part of a healthy lifestyle? One of our health's greatest enemies is stress, and the best antidote to stress is laughter. An antidote is a medicine given to counteract a particular poison. So, in this case, stress is the poison and laughter is the medicine. Have you ever heard the phrase "Laughter is the best medicine"? It's true! Laughter will be our antidote to stress.

Let's talk about stress. You might think that stress is something only adults have, but children can have stress, too. If you've ever had to study for an important test or worked on a school project with a deadline, you might have experienced stress. You could also have stress if there is a problem in your life that hasn't been solved yet or a situation that you're not happy with. Stress is an inevitable part of everyone's life, but it's important that we recognize when we feel stress and not let ourselves stay stressed for long. Remember, stress is the poison and laughter is the medicine that can heal it.

Have you ever laughed so hard that your laugh turned silent? Or have you ever laughed so hard you cried? When we genuinely laugh, we experience strong emotions of joy. Laughter is contagious! I bet the wonderful sound of your laughter makes the people you love want to laugh, too. In this fun section let's explore some challenges and games that will make you laugh. You can turn to these whenever you feel stressed. It's time to take your laughter medicine!

These are just a few ideas of what you can do if you feel sad, bored, or stressed. Play one of these games with people you love, and your whole day will turn around. Allow your laughter to heal you. Connoisseur Kids know that it's OK to be silly! Let yourself have fun, and let your laughter ring out for others to hear.

Stone Face

Play this game with three or more family members or friends. The more, the merrier. One person will be Stone Face, and everyone else will be the jesters. Stone Face must sit down with a straight face and not smile or laugh. The jesters take turns to try to make Stone Face break into a smile. Each jester has 30 seconds. The jesters may not touch Stone Face. If Stone Face smiles or laughs, he or she becomes a jester, and the person who made him or her laugh becomes Stone Face.

Banana Challenge

Gather two or more friends or family members. Each person gets a banana. Take off your socks and shoes. Place your hands behind your back, and try to unpeel the banana with just your toes. The first person with an unpeeled banana wins! Try not to laugh during this game. It's impossible!

Elephant March Game

This game is the definition of silly. Gather your family and friends, and get ready to laugh!

YOU WILL NEED:
Softball or large orange
Pantyhose
10 to 12 water bottles

Place the softball or large orange in the foot of the pantyhose. Place the pantyhose on your head (but make sure you can still breathe). The leg with the ball in it will look like an elephant trunk. Have the water bottles spread out in two rows in front of you. The object of the game is to swing your head and use your "elephant trunk" to knock down the water bottles. You must walk in the middle of the two lanes of water bottles, which will require you to swing your trunk well. You have 1 minute to do this. Take turns using the elephant trunk, and the one who knocks down the most bottles wins.

Dance Chain

This will help you get the wiggles out and your laughing on. The first person does a simple dance move, like the twist. The second person does the twist and then adds a dance move, such as shaking their right foot. The third person does the twist, shakes their right foot, and adds another move, such as jazz hands. Keep going with as many people as are playing until you are all dancing the same crazy long dance!

The Oinking Game

Oh dear, this game is super silly and very funny! One person wears a blindfold. The other people playing have to oink like a pig. The blindfolded person has to guess whose oink belongs to whom.

The Laughing Game

In this game you will take turns asking each other questions. The person answering may only answer with a chosen word or phrase. Sample questions could be: What did you sit on? Where do you live? What do you eat? What's in your pocket? Examples of chosen answers could be: stinky socks, squashed bananas, Granny's underpants. Choose whatever questions you like, and assign whatever chosen answer you like. The key is to not break out into laughter while playing. Very hard to do!

A Last Word on Health

Living a healthy lifestyle is not only rewarding because you will feel better each day, but it's also fun to do. Healthy choices are exciting choices. Picture a life where you spend most of your time hunched over playing video games and eating doughnuts. Ack! While it sounds like it might be fun to do one Saturday afternoon, you would never want to spend your life doing this. You want to be outdoors, active, eating foods that fuel you. You want to be healthy and have vitality. You want to laugh and enjoy life. When you are met with the choice of what to eat or what activity to do, ask yourself which is the healthier one and choose that one. Making healthy choices when you are a Connoisseur Kid will stay with you through your whole life.

THE FUTURE OF CONNOISSEUR KIDS

We have come to the end of our book, and you have learned all about how to be a Connoisseur Kid.

To be a Connoisseur Kid, you strive to be polite, have good table manners, be tidy, have good hygiene, think of other people, eat healthy foods, and get plenty of exercise and rest. Phew! Just thinking about doing all of those things can feel exhausting! Is it even possible to live like that?

A true Connoisseur Kid doesn't do all of those things perfectly, but they always give it their best try and do so with a positive attitude. The main thing to remember to be a true Connoisseur Kid is to just be *you*. Be you, enjoy your life, and always just do your best. All of the lessons you've learned in this book will help you along the way.

You'll have mess-ups and triumphs, good days and bad days, but a true Connoisseur Kid remembers that the most important thing is to have a happy heart. Do everything with a happy heart! When you mess up, just pick yourself up and start again. Tomorrow always holds new opportunities. Keep practicing the ideas in this book, and one day you will realize that they come naturally to you. You will be able to express yourself as a true Connoisseur Kid and inspire others. You are wonderful and important, and your small actions can change the world for the better. So rejoice, and enjoy every step of the journey to becoming a Connoisseur Kid.

THE END

With deep gratitude to my agent, Erica Silverman, and the team at Trident Media Group; my editor, Sarah Billingsley, and the team at Chronicle Books; my friends, the readers, and the viewers of The Daily Connoisseur; and my family, especially my husband and children, who took on each challenge in this book with such gusto. I love you so much. And finally, with thanks and praise to God.

Index